MW01121953

Naked Memory

Confessions of a Sexual Revolutionary

A Memoir by

Dr. Gloria G. Brame

Moons Grove Press
British Columbia, Canada

Naked Memory
Confessions of a Sexual Revolutionary

Copyright ©2014 by Dr. Gloria G. Brame
ISBN-13 978-1-77143-141-5
First Edition

Library and Archives Canada Cataloguing in Publication
Brame, Gloria G., 1955-, author
Naked memory : confessions of a sexual revolutionary
/ by Gloria G. Brame. – First edition.
Issued in print and electronic formats.
ISBN 978-1-77143-141-5 (pbk.).--ISBN 978-1-77143-142-2 (pdf)
Additional cataloguing data available from Library and Archives Canada

Cover photograph credits:
Front cover by Peter Belvin Photography: http://belvinphotography.com
Back cover by Louis Shackleford: http://seductionbylouis.com/

Note: Elements within this memoir have been fictionalized in the interest
of privacy and the author's creative license.

Moons Grove Press is an imprint
of CCB Publishing: www.ccbpublishing.com

Moons Grove Press
British Columbia, Canada
www.moonsgrovepress.com

≥ Contents ≤

&) Preface (&

⌘

I am a surgeon of my own life. I have carved it up without pity. Separated out, the parts are not that pretty. Sewing them back together will take artistry.

Today the experiment begins. I am the surgeon and you are in the operatory where I'll be reanimating specimens and giving them new identities.

As you observe the pieces of my life, and the bones I'm scraping for the first time, I want you to consider this: a heart held by forceps is not the heart that beats, intact, inside a body. When you open old wounds, scar tissue distorts the data. Sometimes, the deeper you go, the less you know.

So let's cut into things.

✂ Everyone Fucks ✂

⌘

My first conscious awareness that adults had sex together occurred spontaneously, without warning, in the most ordinary and typical of childhood ways. I heard it from a friend.

I was standing outside my elementary school, P.S. 169 in Sunset Park, Brooklyn, when my friend Carol casually asked me if I knew how babies were made. I had just devoured a big greasy slice of pizza and the question made me queasy. I was 11 years old and puberty was making a loud and early entrance in my life. My breasts were growing, I'd started menstruating earlier that year and I was noticing boys in ways I never had before. I was starting to separate the ones I liked from the ones I didn't in my mind, and beginning to notice which ones were the cutest or smartest.

Yet though I was filled with romantic daydreams based on the novels and movies I'd read and seen, the mechanics of baby-making eluded me. I was content to leave it that way. It didn't seem like a subject I'd ever need to know about. Even then, I knew I didn't want children. The one time I'd asked my mother why she had children, she told me, "That's what you do when you grow up." It never seemed like a good enough reason to me.

Still, now that Carol raised the subject, curiosity got the better of me. "How?"

Too much info immediately spilled. I felt almost personally insulted by her frank revelation that a man put his thing in a woman's thing. Those were my parents she was talking about! It was a sickening accusation.

"That's disgusting!" I said.

She was a sharp-faced, brainy mouse of a girl. "That's how it is. My mother told me." She smirked. "Better get used to the idea."

Her mother taught school in another district. If her mother told her that, it had to be true.

"No!" I said. "Not my father! NO!"

My kind, handsome father had put that disgusting dirty horrible thing between his legs into my evil mother's more disgusting dirty horrible thing, not just once or twice but at least four times, the number of times my mother had been pregnant: once for the baby brother who died, once for my sister, once for a miscarriage, and once for me. GROSS.

It had only been a few months since I'd first looked up the word "penis" in a dictionary at my sister's house. I saw the word in one of my novels, but couldn't figure out its meaning. It seemed oddly scientific among the flowery novelistic phrases. When I asked my normally voluble and much older brother-in-law about it, he turned ten shades of red and handed me a dictionary before striding quickly out of the room. His embarrassment only piqued my interest in the word penis. What was this mysterious word that could make grown men blush and flee?

Unfortunately, the dictionary shrouded the definition in such baroque clinical language that I wasn't really clear on its meaning until our teacher finally solved the mystery in a biology lesson about fish reproduction. The truth was such an anti-climax. OH. PENIS. I'd been to the Brooklyn Museum. I'd seen the naked Greek statues, and knew men had little dangly marshmallows between their legs. I just didn't know there was a name for those things. Penis. OK. Yuck. Whatever.

I was not raised sex-positive. Early on, my parents instilled a deep fear in me of anything unsanitary, with an emphasis on avoiding the germ-infested pit of ordure that was "down there." Discussion of anything and everything below the waist was forbidden. As my mother often repeated, "Nice people don't think about that." There was no woowoo or veejay or other childish term for my vagina. Penis and vagina did not exist in my parents' vocabulary, which, naturally, only made genitals fascinating to me.

Once the shock wore off from Carol's revelation that men and women joined genitals during sex, and despite my initial revulsion at the thought that my parents did something so freakishly unsanitary together, I began to come around. Since that was how you had babies, and since there were children everywhere you went – I mean, even your own parents and their parents were children once! – it could only mean one thing.

Everyone fucked. Even dead people once did it and now their children and their children's children were doing it too.

So, I reasoned, if everyone did it, if respectable Jewish people like my parents and grandparents did it, perhaps this fucking wasn't so bad. If it was something all adults did, then one day I'd do it too. It was hard to fathom because I didn't have strong urges yet, but I accepted what seemed to be a universal, eternal truth: fucking is human destiny. That meant it was my destiny too.

Perhaps. I had my doubts. I wasn't like other people. I wanted to be, but for whatever reason, I was born to be weird.

❧ Weird Girls ☙ Get Lonely Too

⌘

When I was five, the school principal, Mr. Edelstein, a short, dapper man in horn-rimmed glasses, pulled my mother aside one day when we were leaving the building. According to some standardized tests, I scored higher than any student on record. I was a genius. My mother needed to make special plans for me. Did she understand? He kept talking and repeated that I was a genius while my mother stared at him in disbelief. Mr. Edelstein walked away abruptly, waving his arms. When we left, I asked her what he meant. I knew the word but I was as incredulous as Mom that he used it to apply to me.

"It means you're smart. But don't tell anyone," she said, tugging my hand hard. "It'll only make your sister feel bad. It doesn't mean you're smarter than other people. Don't get a big head."

I agreed. That made more sense than what the principal said. My mother filed it away in her big box of things she couldn't deal with at the moment, and my life as someone who wasn't smarter than other people went on.

From my point of view, if I was a genius I was the dumbest genius that ever lived. Everyone was cooler than me. Other kids seemed to know how things worked. They dressed nicer and they smelled better too. They knew unspoken rules and keys to success. Most of all, they knew how to BE, un-self-consciously, as if life came naturally to them. They didn't lie in bed all night every night, too agitated to sleep, worrying about the galaxy exploding, thinking every car alarm was an air raid siren, or fantasizing about being held captive in the time of the Roman gladiators. They didn't continually make contingency plans in their head for every possible manner of emergency, from getting stranded without bus fare to a nuclear holocaust.

I wasn't a genius. I was a weirdo. Everywhere I went people could see the weirdness vibrating out of me. I tried to keep my inner self under wraps, which meant toning myself down for public consumption and being quieter in public than in private. Anything I might say or do could open me to scrutiny as someone who didn't feel or think like other kids my age, who didn't listen to the same music or share the same ambitions.

It didn't always work. Sometimes kids picked on me and excluded me from cliques, and I always knew it was because they sensed my inner Weird. To be honest, I didn't have a high opinion of them either but the peer pressure to conform tormented me. I desperately wanted to be another normal girl who could fly under life's radar.

My real life was an inner world that no one could penetrate. That was the only way my thoughts and feelings could run free, and no one but me would ever know of my extreme passions and bizarre fantasies. I learned to sit in class while conducting long inner monologues; I learned to sit with my parents and travel the world in my head. Through hopscotch games, summer camps, and class trips, I went through all the motions while watching myself watch myself be. It was easy to hide in plain sight.

Still, weird girls get lonely too. I was eleven when I spontaneously invited someone into my secret world of extreme passion and profound emotion. Walter was the most attractive boy at school, maybe the most handsome boy I had ever seen. Even today I remember the enchanted aura of his beauty. He was a latte-colored boy with the softest, fuzziest brown hair, burning black eyes and an intensely serious attitude about everything. He was a rebel, a bona fide bad boy. He wore hand-me-down shirts and hi-top sneakers. He'd been left back for juvenile delinquency and led a loyal gang of baby thugs, including a wall-eyed boy who was rumored to be a grave robber.

As a nice nerdy girl in the Intellectually Gifted program at school, a girl who'd always followed all the rules, Walter was everything I was not. He was beautiful and I was plain. He was tall, lean, athletic and self-confident; I was a short, shy, chunky girl who constantly apologized. I stared at him in the schoolyard, and he was soon at my side, relaxed and shining his pearly teeth at me. He walked me halfway home that day. He told me I had a nice shape, making the two-handed sign of the peanut in the air. I was speechless with joy. I had a shape?!

No one had ever talked to me like this. He was thirteen and a man of the world. Just the older man I had fantasized about – handsome, intelligent and worlds away from everything and everyone familiar. When we were alone, he was the soft-spoken one, and hung on every word I said.

Overnight, our souls merged. The next day, I was in love with Walter and he was in love with me. We understood one another as much as we needed to. We hooked up daily after the final bell, meeting behind a staircase near a seldom-used emergency exit. There, holding our breath to listen for footsteps, I kissed him the way I'd seen people do it in movies. I crammed my lips so tight against his he couldn't breathe. When he pulled away I grabbed him tighter. For reasons I couldn't explain, sometimes I punched his back hard while we clutched in tight embrace. I didn't know where the impulse came from but I wanted to see him react when I hurt him that way.

When I landed a particularly painful blow, he'd gasp, tears springing to his dark eyes, and ask, "Why? Why do you do that?"

I never had an answer. I didn't know why. I'd just start kissing him again, harder.

It didn't take too long for rumors to spread about our interracial romance. Since I grew up around the extended black family of my childhood best friend Ruby, and since her people came in all colors, from tan to midnight, to me Walter was just a gorgeous boy whose skin color made him even cuter. But working class Brooklyn was not liberal-minded about racial differences. One of his female cousins, a notoriously mean thug-ette, threatened to beat me up because she didn't think a white Jewgirl should date a Negro boy. She said I was ruining her cousin's reputation. Walter was embarrassed by her drama, and escorted me out of school when the bell rang with his gang trailing us as security until he finally got her cooled down.

It was my sixth grade teacher who delivered the hurtful blow. I idolized my teacher, Mr. Isaacs, a pious Jewish man who seemed to have a heart of gold for children, and doted on the six Jewish kids in the class as if we were his own. I didn't realize until much later that the only thing that matched his affection for his Jewish students was his disinterest in the non-Jewish ones.

When rumor of my dalliance with Walter finally reached his ears, he felt compelled to talk to me about it, as my moral guide.

"I'm very disappointed in you," he said. "I expect you to stop seeing him. Nice Jewish girls don't associate with *them*."

I was crushed by his criticism but enraged. I expected racism from the uneducated kids in the neighborhood, not from an adult who acted so pious and refined. His racism steeled my determination to rise above it all. Fuck you, Mr. Isaacs. Walter and I would be together forever. Nothing would ever keep us apart.

That is, until a few short weeks later when Walter told me his mother had decided to move the family to Florida before school started up again. The news was so awful it left us speechless. We stood outside P.S. 169, gazing silently like two wounded baby deer into each other's eyes. We knew we were fucked. We had no control over where we lived. We were pawns in our parents' lives.

Walter reached into his jeans pocket and handed me a brooch. He got it from his mother's jewelry box. He wanted me to have it. It was beautiful and adult. I accepted it, crying. It was over, just like that. No more passionate hugs from his strong skinny arms, no more endless kisses with our bodies pressed tight, no more punches, and no more co-conspirator in my secret life. I was all alone with myself again.

I trudged home that day and threw myself dramatically onto my bed to languish in my not entirely unpleasant misery. It was the first time that I felt the pain of love. I kind of liked it. The idea that I'd had my first grown-up-style affair, with star-crossed lovers and racial tensions and all kinds of dramatic novelistic details made my pubertal brain spin. A love like this, I decided, deserved a long and tragic period of mourning.

I spent two weeks lying on my bed and listening to the Johnny Mathis album *Open Fire, Two Guitars* hundreds of times. A few days before my 12th birthday, I shut the stereo, and went outside to play ball. Grieving was boring. I knew the words to all the songs on the album backward and forward. There were only a couple of weeks until school started up again. I'd spent the entire summer in my room, thinking about the meaning of love and the romantic adventures I wanted to have, and how amazing it was to have a beautiful companion in my secret life, someone who knew I was weird but liked me anyway.

There had to be others. I would miss Walter but my life with boys and men had just begun. Sixth grade was over. I was starting Junior High. I would meet new boys, I would find joy in other boys' arms, I would have trysts in other dark corners with all kinds of boys, and they would kiss me and love me the way Walter did.

I couldn't wait. I wanted to live for love, like the heroines in great books do.

❧ The Bleeding, ❧ the Orthodox Bra, and the Art of French Kissing

⌘

Until Carol told me about intercourse, I lived in a kind of blur of false impressions and torrid fantasies that stopped at the waist because I honestly didn't know what lay below the waist. Though I'd been touching myself for years, I did it in the dark, and usually with a blanket or an object of some kind. But I wanted to learn. I desperately wanted to know why sex was such a big deal in all the books I read, and how grown-ups actually loved together. The timing of Carol's revelation was fortuitous. Once I knew people fucked, other things started falling into place, albeit with some loud crashing noises along the way. Puberty was upon me like a beast and my brain was scrambling to keep up with all the new events and eye-openers.

I was around age ten and a half, sitting in fifth grade homeroom, when my lower stomach started feeling funny. I asked for the pass to the girls' bathroom and when I got into the stall and pulled down my panties I saw blood in the crotch.

That was it. I was dying. I was bleeding out. Something had gone tragically wrong. My innards were falling out. I would never see my family again.

I ran back to class in a panic, and approached the teacher's desk.

"Yes?"

I whispered urgently. "I'm dying."

She arched her penciled-in eyebrows and asked why I'd say that, yet continued grading papers as if children said that to her every day. When I told her about the blood, she reached for the key to the teachers' bathroom in her desk drawer, handed it to me and told me to go there and wait. She was calling the principal's office. She told me not to worry.

She didn't seem as alarmed as I'd expected. If I wasn't dying, what was it? I walked back down the hall and unlocked the teachers' bathroom. I felt better once I was inside. It was cleaner and quieter than the student toilets. It felt very adult to be in there. My teacher wouldn't just send me off to die alone, would she?

A school secretary opened the door and handed me something wrapped in paper. "Use this," she whispered, scurrying back out the door.

Now this really was a mystery. I opened the paper and inside was a big surgical pad. I cleaned myself and my undies as best I could, discarded it and went back to my classroom. The teacher told me to stand beside her while she marked papers and tersely explained the mysteries of womanhood to me.

"When a girl becomes a woman, her body changes," she said. "Her womb fills up with poison and then, once a month, it has to get rid of that poison or she'll get sick," she said. "It lasts a week, and then it will happen again every month from now on."

I returned to my desk in shock. What the fuck was this? I was a bearer of poison and I was going to bleed from my vagina for the rest of my life? Was she serious?

By the time I was back in my seat, it seemed like all my class-mates already knew.

"You better wear a sweater, girl," my seatmate, Ellery, whispered nervously to me. "You are going to bleed so bad all your clothes will be covered with blood. You better bring a sweater to tie around your waist. I heard about this girl, she got her period once, and when she stood up from her seat, there was blood dripping on the floor." She leaned in. "Are you wearing a double pad?"

Holy shit! I was supposed to wear it? I threw my pad away. She scared me so much, I asked permission to leave school early, and ran home clutching my books over my groin.

The school called my mother to give her the update, so by the time I reached home, she was waiting for me.

"Mazel tov," she said. "You're a woman now."

"I am?" I was flabbergasted.

"No, not really," she said.

We faced each other across the old gray formica table. She admitted that the doctor told her a few months earlier that I'd probably start menstruating soon. I couldn't believe she'd kept this to herself. Why didn't she tell me? She shrugged and looked away. The doctor said she should but she didn't think I was ready to know.

But I sensed this was going to be my big adult conversation about sex, so I didn't argue. I had a million questions. But there was only one I was sure my mother knew the answer to, and that was the business of babies. How did men and women actually make babies?

Her face fell. "I don't know," she finally said. "Is there anything else?" she asked.

"Nah, I'm good," I said. She wasn't going to tell me anything. I knew it. It was pointless to play this game with her.

"Good." She stood up, relieved. "Your sister will talk to you more tonight."

My sister did as ordered and showed me how to use a pad and dispose of it, even giving me an old sanitary belt of hers to get me started. But neither she nor my mother said a word about sex or any of the changes I should expect in my body or my feelings about boys.

Getting my period, however, must have jostled my mother's consciousness though because, a few weeks later, she announced that it was time to take me to get fitted for a brassiere. I knew my shirts were getting tighter but I was too shy to look at myself naked in the mirror and went blank in the shower. I didn't want to think about what was happening to me and so I didn't, other than a persistent sense that my body was at war with my mind. Growing pains burned in my legs and my chest. I didn't want breasts. I definitely didn't want to bleed. Other girls my age were flat-chested and poison-free. Next, pimples started popping on me. My body wanted to destroy me.

By fifth grade, the bumps on my chest were growing so fast that my girlfriend Gina asked if she could measure me every week to chart my breast progress. She was a charmingly impish Italian girl, a year ahead of me in school, and seemed to know much more about sexual development than me. So I let her, because I shared her scientific curiosity about the beast that was overtaking me. It made me feel a little better that at least someone was enjoying the experience. As for me, at the rate they were going, I was afraid my breasts would never stop growing.

Unfortunately, Gina's fascination with my breast growth was accompanied by an affection I couldn't deal with. One day, she said she wanted to call me "Mommy." At first, I agreed and for weeks we were "Mommy" and "Baby" when we were alone. But after a sleepover at her house, crammed with her into a single bed under a large and terrifying crucifix with the Savior splayed and suffering, a sight that always deeply disturbed me, when she wanted to kiss me and feel my breasts while calling me "Mommy," I resolved it was all too weird for me and stopped inviting her home.

My body was turning me into a sexpot I didn't want to be and bringing me new ways to suffer. Now my mother was buying me skirts and dresses instead of the pants I preferred to wear. I hated the slips and the stockings and the pantygirdles she insisted I put on at age 11. I hated make-up; the smell of hairspray made me gag. Pretending to cook invisible meals or feed a plastic baby bored the shit out of me. Every doll I owned ended up dissected, injected and otherwise tortured in macabre experiments to find out how they looked inside. I turned to my father's old clothes as salvation – sleeping in his t-shirts, wearing his tattered dress shirts and even his ties, anything to avoid the wretchedly uncomfortable trappings of 1960s femininity.

But now, thanks to puberty, in addition to a monthly torture belt and stinky pad, I'd have to wear something strapped tight around my chest every day. I'd seen the painful red welts on my mother's shoulders from the cheap cotton bras that held up her huge breasts. DOOM. I was doomed.

She told me to put on a coat, and walked me to the Orthodox section of our neighborhood. She was zealously atheistic and shunned Chasidim as ridiculously old-fashioned and backwards. But for this purpose, she led me to a cramped little store on

13th Avenue in the heart of Jewy Jewville where she and a rabbi-looking man in a black coat and long beard talked familiarly about my developing breasts.

It was the worst five minutes of my puberty. I tuned them out. I didn't want to hear. A few minutes later, he gently shook my arm. He asked me to ball up my hand. My mother nodded at me knowingly as he carefully measured my fist with slow precision.

"That's how to measure for a bra," she said. "They know from your fist what your cup size is."

Well, that sounded crazy. I already knew my breasts weren't fist-sized. They were more Mallomar size, as recent chart calculations by Gina suggested. I couldn't tell my mother that Gina had been measuring my breasts and had more reliable results so I just kept quiet and let the adults do their thing.

"She needs a trainer bra." He turned to the massive wood shelves behind him and removed two slim white boxes, setting them on the glass counter. "She should wear this." He opened one dramatically. "Or she should wear this." He presented the other as if it was a Hermes scarf. He beamed over his merchandise, tenderly fingering the lace on the bras, cajoling my mother to buy them both, perhaps sensing that she pinched her purse tighter than a dominatrix squeezes balls yet determined to close the sale.

I fought back the million deaths of embarrassment that puberty brings. I couldn't stand it that this religious Jew even KNEW I had breasts.

To add insult to injury, when I got home the bra didn't fit. I spent the next few months fighting to keep the bra's straps from popping every time I ran or jumped until my mother grudgingly admitted it was the wrong size. For the next purchase, she took me to Alexander's Department Store, and let me pick one out myself.

And so it went, a stumbling and bumbling little journey through puberty, with boys and girls weaving through my life for reasons that usually made me profoundly uneasy, from the boys who tried to feel me up when I didn't want them to, to the girls who kissed me until I literally couldn't take it. I didn't judge them. I was just developing my own sense of the things that I liked and the things that I didn't. When it came to boys, I realized, I pretty much liked kissing all the good-looking ones, and was always disappointed if a boy I spent alone time with didn't at least try to kiss me first.

By age 12 ½, I considered myself an expert on kissing. But when a European family, old friends of my parents, stayed with us that spring, their 19-year-old son blew my mind. Marek was sober, reserved, and seemed more mature than American boys his age. He had short curly dark blonde hair, a red moustache and a long nose and he wore geeky polyester pants and flat black shoes, which instantly turned me off. He was very intelligent, though, and very polite. We spent a couple of evenings together alone in my room while the adults chatted in the kitchen. His English was rocky, so it was hard to communicate. But I understood immediately when he leaned in for a kiss. I wasn't really into him but there was no denying he was nice looking.

At first, his moustache was scratchy. Then, he opened his lips wide and stuck his tongue inside my mouth.

"EUW!" I recoiled. "What are you doing? EUW!"

"Is called Frrrench Kissink," he said calmly. "Is khow adults kiss."

I had heard the term but had only the vaguest notion of what it meant. I had never seen my parents kiss like that, that's for sure. I was positive that if I asked, they'd tell me it was disgusting. They didn't have to tell me. A deep-rooted fear of germs was second to my Jewish nature and what could be more infectious than swapping saliva. A tongue in a stranger's mouth? FEH! How could anyone do that?

Marek said it was normal, it's what people did, especially when they were turned on by someone. This set me back. Was Marek saying I turned him on?

I squelched my repulsion.

"You want I should teach you khow?" he asked.

"Okay," I said. If that was how adults did it, I had to learn!

I let him move his tongue around in my mouth until I felt nauseous. At the end, he smiled at me, and I felt like I'd just sexually matured by several years.

The next day, I told my friend Diana. She was even more excited than me.

"You French Kissed! OMG. What was it like, what was it like?"

"It was DISGUSTING!" I said. "It was the most disgusting thing I've ever done."

"Really? I don't know. It sounds kind of sexy," Diana said.

"Euw. But I did it."

"You did. Wow," she said with admiration in her voice.

It got me thinking. Of all the sex things I'd heard about thus far, the tongue thing was the slimiest, strangest and most germ-laden of all. Before Marek, I could have sworn I'd never do something so gross. But in memory it seemed kind of sexy and really intimate to be orally connected to someone. Sharing juiciness like that was kind of delightful, in fact. Marek was so sweet too. After that kiss, I forgot about his Euro-geekiness and could only remember how beautiful his face looked in profile and how cute his chest was.

It taught me that you never know what might be sexy in bed until you try it. It was also the last time in my life that I ever felt disgusted by a sexual act.

ℬ Miss Bliss ℭ

⌘

Although the concept of intercourse interested me, it also scared me. I knew I wasn't ready for it, but I also knew I was dying to be close to boys so I could kiss them and be held by them. Since Walter, I hadn't been steady with anyone and despite a lot of random encounters, felt completely alone once more. I had crushes on older boys who barely noticed me, boys my own age were obnoxious, and puberty had now brought me to the teetering edge of full-blown adolescence, where each day was a new and deeper pit of hellish self-consciousness, self-loathing and almost untenable horniness.

Seventh grade was virtually bereft of boys. Instead, I focused most of my energy on my friendship with my classmate Diana who, two years later, would tell me that she was bisexual. Diana was a social outsider and reject like me at school, but it only made her one of the coolest kids in the school. She had incredible fashion sense and a great figure, plus she was a talented artist. We were so close that, for a time, we were like extensions of each other – finishing each other's thoughts, and shutting others out, like twins who speak their own private language. Most of our conversation focused on a long, euw-filled critical review of all the boys and male teachers at school. We did not give them high marks. We preferred each other's company.

I lusted after a male Social Science teacher, literally obsessed with his bulging pants and overwhelmed with curiosity about what a penis look liked. I also became involved in a profoundly romantic but chaste relationship with a female Biology teacher, Bliss.

It was unexpected and cool to be the teacher's pet. Teachers sometimes favored me because I scored so high on things, but Bliss immediately let me know that she treasured me for my soul. That was so poetic it immediately entranced me. With every passing week, Bliss and I grew closer; she was a strict Catholic, but took a special interest in this peculiar Jewish girl. Every night, she wrote me a long letter in neat cursive on expensive, perfumed stationery, and every day, she would discreetly hand it to me in class when other kids couldn't see.

I was at the peak of early adolescent drama, and grappling with depression and suicidal thoughts. Bliss was the perfect co-conspirator for my fantasy that I was the tragic heroine of my own life. I'd scrawl long, incoherent screeds about my agonies. She began calling me "Little One," and reacted with religious fervor to my laments. The more emotional she became about my welfare, the more embarrassed I felt because it wasn't entirely real to me. I didn't really want to kill myself. I knew other kids had it a lot worse. She didn't really need to worry about me, I'd be okay. Still, her tender concern was balm to me and I could not stop basking in it.

Bliss also told me stories about her long-time boyfriend and how, as good Catholics, they never consummated. I found it weird when she'd describe how sexually riled up they'd get only to back away just when they craved each other the most. I didn't understand how you could want someone and not take the next logical step. To Bliss it was self-evident: nice people did not have sex before marriage. I had already figured out that nice people did, but I didn't contradict her because I was so flattered that she confided the details of her sex life to me, as if I was an adult. Besides, I never let religion get in the way.

My parents were atheists. Everyone's belief systems sounded absurd to me, but it seemed like everyone had one so I kept my opinions to myself.

Despite our obvious differences in age and beliefs, I thought Bliss was an angel to care so much for someone like me. Bliss took me for ice cream sodas, drove me around in her flashy red Dodge Charger and taught me to play "Freight Train" on the guitar. I couldn't believe that someone was so nice to me for no apparent reason, and I glugged from her copious fountain of affection with selfish abandon, embroidering my notes with a pathos and tragedy I didn't really feel.

Still, I was a little timid when she invited me to visit her home over the Easter break. I wasn't in her class that semester and had seen very little of her. Now I had to make special trips to her room to exchange notes, and it felt awkward. I'd never gone to an adult's house by myself before. On impulse, I stopped at Diana's house on the way over and made her come along with me. It was a bleak and frigid day, and we hurried through the barren streets, hands dug deep into the pockets of our thin coats.

Bliss opened the door slowly, checked us out, a surly look on her face.

"I brought Diana, is that okay?"

"Oh," she said, turning away to go back inside and leaving the door open for us. We followed her in mutely.

Although I'd arranged a time and day with her by phone, it looked as if she wasn't expecting anyone. She was still dressed in her pajamas and they were weirdly slutty – more like a frilly pink babydoll nightie with disturbingly short matching pink bottoms that displayed her legs to spectacularly poor advantage. She was rather plain and had thick mannish legs you didn't notice as much in long skirts. Now she was almost naked.

The living room was dark, and Bliss walked ahead of us and sat silently on the couch. She pushed a half-eaten box of half-melted chocolates at me. I tried to make small talk but I couldn't get a word out of her. Diana was fidgeting beside me, whispering in my ear, "This is so boring. When can we leave?"

I don't know what Bliss had in mind. Perhaps she hoped to seduce me until she saw my fresh-faced friend behind me and got pissed because I'd ruined the opportunity. Perhaps she went on a drunk the night before and forgot all about our appointment, and was annoyed at having to deal with kids during her hangover. I was relieved that I had Diana with me, and felt like I'd escaped something weirdly unpleasant when I got us back out the door.

"What was that?" Diana asked as we walked back.

"Off day," I shrugged, "she's usually really nice."

I was never naïve about sex but I didn't want to upset Diana, so I just put the event away in my mind. Diana had no clue what had just happened and never asked about it again. I stopped dropping by Bliss' classroom and her notes stopped abruptly.

As for Diana, the day she told me she was bisexual, we kissed and kissed for an hour, as I tried to figure out if I might be bisexual too. I wanted to be, if only to cement my friendship with her forever, but her thin lips were hard and sharp, nothing like Walter's soft wide sensual ones. I was on top of her, kissing her with genuine emotion, but her frame felt too tiny, too frail and I finally rolled off, mystified. Our failure to physically connect was a let-down for us both, and the friendship began to drift. The next year, she went to a high school for the arts, and we lost touch forever.

❦ The Circus ❧
We Never Joined

⌘

Pershing Junior High put me in an accelerated learning program called "special progress." You got to skip eighth grade, which thrilled me because it put me one year closer to being an adult.

Owing either to the meanness or incompetence – likely both – that was my junior high's administrative staff, they separated me and Diana in ninth grade, and put me in a strangely unbalanced class of six girls and 25 hormonally overwrought boys who routinely had spitball fights. The homeroom teacher sequestered the girls in a corner, which at least offered the strategic advantage of being out of range of the slimy missiles that scattered among the boys whenever the homeroom teacher turned her back.

Then one day, I noticed...him. A blonde god. A movie star. Bright ruby lips and eyes as clear as blue glass. Like Walter, he was tall and lean, and all sharp angles. He was so white, my pupils shrank. At my first opportunity, I passed him a note. I have no idea what I said, but it was enough to make him write a note back. His name was Timothy.

And thus began my first texting relationship – the 1960s version anyway. We had few opportunities to meet outside of class at first, but in class we were note-writing demons. And since the class was French, our subject soon turned to romance.

"J'aime tu," we'd write each other back and forth as fast as our Bic pens could scribble. (If we'd been listening to the teacher we might have known it should've been "je t'aime.") Once, for some class project, the teacher moved us far apart and we had to depend on a loyal network of friends to silently pass the notes along under tables and across aisles.

It wasn't just a physical attraction. Timothy was a poet and so was I. We wrote poems to each other, for each other, about each other. We were going to run away and be poets together. Perhaps we'd join a circus and travel the world together, writing poetry that was raw and real and full of the experiences we would have.

I remember our first tryst vividly. It was the winter holidays, and the pain of being parted for two whole weeks drove us crazy. We came up with a plan – we would leave the neighborhood and go adventuring together. We both lied to our parents and surreptitiously met at an out-of-the-way subway station, taking the train to Prospect Park. It was only a few subway stops away but it felt like Paris to us. No one knew us there. No one could stop our love. We owned our world.

Everything was frozen solid as far as the eye could see. The world was white and gray. My feet were so numb it felt as if I was walking on packs of frozen steaks. Timothy had hurried ahead and come to a stop by a tree, where he tried to shield himself from the cutting winds to wait for me.

My father was a tailor of coats, so I always had good winter clothes. That day, I wore socks and boots and a heavy wool coat and gloves and a scarf and a hat, and still I was shivering. Timothy wore jeans, sneakers, a thin shirt, and a corduroy jacket. His lips were almost blue. The sleeves of his hand-me-down jacket were too short, and his wrists and hands were lobster red. I saw him tug his sleeves to cover his wrists when I came to him. My heart melted for him, how cold and helpless he looked just then. I threw myself into his arms and, for the first time, we kissed. I felt his heartbeat through his thin clothes, and pressed in even closer to spread my body's warmth. I would have stayed with him under that tree until spring, is how I felt then.

Some romances are destined to last forever. My romance with Timothy reached its apogee under that barren tree in Prospect Park. I sensed we wouldn't last, and that knowledge didn't make me sad. I'd felt the same with Walter. There's always more to life than who you are with right now, there's who you could be with tomorrow.

Even as Timothy and I continued our furtive kissing dates, and our constant flow of poetic notes, I felt restless and consumed by other boys. As would happen to me so very often through my teens and twenties, once the blush was off the lust, my feelings would ebb and retreat until the same embraces that I plunged into only last night now felt like unpleasant invasions of my personal space.

In the background of my lusts was an older boy, Martin, 17 to my 12. I believed Martin might be my one true love, that "one true love" that novelists always wrote about. Frankly, it was hard to imagine there being only *one,* given how many different boys intrigued me and drew my eye. But if there WAS that one special ONE, I was hungry to establish that fact and get on with our life as a pair. Meanwhile, though, it only made sense to explore as much as I could before I settled down with Martin. Love and sex, as I understood them, were good things. From my extensive reading of French and Russian novels, that's what made adults the happiest. I wanted to be happy like that.

The following year, Timothy and I went to different high schools, making meetings even more difficult than before. Once, when my mom was on a shopping trip, I invited him home and we kissed all afternoon. We had stripped down to underwear, but I was as yet too shy to take a peek or even touch him "down there." I did a good job pretending his lower anatomy wasn't there until I noticed that a greasy wet spot had oozed onto his bright white BVDs. I had no idea what it was, and he seemed embarrassed by it, so I got embarrassed too. We quickly dressed, just in time for my mother to return home.

The year after that, my parents moved to Sheepshead Bay. Geography made dates too difficult for me. We had to take a subway and three city buses to meet. But he did visit me once. He traveled almost two hours to see my new life in a neighborhood of trees and parks and comfortable brick homes, nothing like the treacherous area where I'd grown up and he still lived.

My parents were away, and I'd moved into their bedroom for the duration. We sat side by side, searching for conversation, but things weren't the same anymore. We began making out passionately, but something was off there too. Our excitement quickly dwindled and turned back to conversation.

It was impossible to disguise our rift. My life had changed for the better in a bourgeois neighborhood filled with hippies who welcomed me into their cliques and I was having erotic adventures left and right. I was in the honors program at my high school and couldn't wait to start college. Timothy was in trouble – he wasn't doing well at school, and life in the old neighborhood and at home kept getting worse. He was angry, depressed, and, at 17, already tired of living.

Before he left, he told me he couldn't stay in Brooklyn anymore. He was quitting high school. He was running away from home. He was going to join that circus we talked about. He told me I would never see him again.

I felt like such a fraud then. Here I was, the rebel, the revolutionary, the runaway, settled into a cozy middle class life. I even had an allowance now and could afford to treat him to a burger at McDonald's. I was a sellout. Timothy was the true rebel in the end, the working class poet who would fulfill the dreams I didn't have the courage, or even the urge anymore, to pursue. We kissed goodbye like war-torn lovers at a train station, one going off to face uncertainty, the other left to ponder the safety she had chosen.

Timothy was wrong, though. I did see him again. I think he wished I didn't, but I did.

It was about a dozen years after that dramatic parting. I was working at Morgan Stanley as a financial analyst, now married and living in the Bronx. I'd been a Wall Street analyst for several years by then and had the program down. Business suit, check. Designer shoes, check. Fine jewelry, check. Leather briefcase in one hand, *Wall Street Journal* in the other, check.

I darted into Au Bon Pain for my morning coffee and roll. Ahead of me, I saw a familiar face and shape in a heavy denim jacket. It looked like Timothy. In the chaos of morning rush, the place was jammed, and I couldn't get to him. Then, before I knew it, he vanished. I went to work that day wondering if it was just my imagination, but began making a habit of getting to Au Bon Pain at the same time for the next week.

It finally paid off. He was already in line when I got inside one morning. The place was having a lull, making it easy to get to him. I was still a few steps behind him when he swirled to face me as if he had eyes in the back of his head.

"I thought it was you," he said.

"Timothy? Oh my God, Timothy, how are you?"

He looked at my briefcase. "You're doing well," he said.

Was his voice tinged by anger? Contempt? Or was it envy?

He looked like hell. His face was bloated, his eyes puffy and lined with creases, his skin sallow. He looked ten years older than me. I saw a thousand nights of hard drinking written all over him.

"What are you doing here?" I asked.

"I'm working construction at a site across the street." He repeated it as if I didn't understand what that meant. "I'm a construction worker."

"Oh!" I was more self-conscious by the second. What had happened to him? And what had happened to me? We were once one soul; now we could barely speak.

"It's so good to see you," I lied, scrambling for words. "Did you...did you ever join the circus?"

And then for a brief second, he was Timothy again. "No," he said, "no, I stayed."

Then he sneered. "I have kids now," he said, holding up two fingers. "I have kids. Do you have kids?"

"No," I shook my head, "I don't have any."

"I have two," he snapped. "Two boys."

"You must be proud."

"Yeah!" he said, looking angry.

"Well that's great," I said. "I'll probably never have kids."

He seemed vaguely mollified when I said that. Then he was gone. And that really was the last time I saw Timothy.

❧ The Dark Undertow ❧

⌘

hen I said that I was never naïve about sex, I meant it. I
was ignorant, but never naïve.

I was the child of Holocaust Survivors. Not a day of my childhood went by that I wasn't reminded of the losses we had suf-
fered at the hands of monsters who committed unfathomable
atrocities against millions of human beings. I can't remember
learning about Concentration Camps because I can't remember
a time I didn't know they had existed. I can't remember learning about mothers having babies killed before their eyes, and
people thrown into mass graves because, again, that knowledge was fed to me with my pabulum and into my marrow.

I knew. I always knew. I knew that anyone, any time, even the
person who was the most doting parent or animal lover could –
because of some unrevealed moral flaw – turn into a murder-
ous beast. I can't say that it bothered me much either, because
I just accepted it the way you accept earthquakes or floods. It
wasn't personal. I couldn't stop it. Predators were part of the
landscape of life. Your only choice was to keep your guard up
and be ready to run at a moment's notice.

Most of my childhood was spent in the clutch of my parents'
circle of Holocaust Survivors and their children. Survivors' children were different from everyone else. We thought about
what the Nazis did to our families all the time. We'd seen the
blue numbers stamped on flesh, not in movies or in books but

on the arms of our relatives and their friends. We were all the children of our parents' new lives, lives they never planned to have in a country they never planned to inhabit, and we were the children many of them had to compensate for the children and relatives they lost to Hitler. We were, in a sense, shadow children, living in the shadow of the Holocaust and its devastation on our parents' emotional lives.

I would say, all in all, it suited me quite well for a life of sexual misadventures.

As early as I remember, sex was part of my life. I didn't actually know it was sex when I was little, I just knew that soft sensations between my legs felt amazingly great. I was very fond of straddling a hard chair and riding it like a pony for hours; I really enjoyed squatting under the dripping faucet in the bathroom too to feel the icy drops slithering down over my perineum. That there was a place on my body that gave me instant pleasure, and that I could control my moods and personal happiness just by rubbing it, changed my emotional outlook. There was relief from the agony of life! Natural relief! My vagina was like a drug pump – a couple of taps and I felt better.

I don't know when encounters with strangers began. From conscious memory, I can date it from the spanking party affair at my elderly aunt's house during a Passover Seder when I was about 7 or 8 years old. I was the oldest of the young children, but still several years younger than the adolescents, so I got locked away with a pack of rambunctious second cousins. It was awfully boring until one of them suggested that we have a spanking party, and that each of them would take a turn being spanked.

This sounded like the stupidest idea I'd ever heard until they unanimously decided I was the one who should do the spanking. That was better and I was curious, so I sat in a chair, while the three or four cousins lined up, dropped their pants or raised their skirts, and propped their tiny behinds on my lap. I remember that one child had a particularly clammy bottom and my palm sort of stuck to it a little, which disgusted me. I realize there are some who would qualify that as their first BDSM experience. I scratch it off to "the crazy stuff kids do without adult supervision."

But my first conscious dealings with boys started around age eight or nine, and, in a sense, I have the Holocaust to thank for that. My parents' friends were all fellow immigrants and Survivors; they were afraid of Americans. They clung to their clique of broken-hearted Polish and Russian Jews whose unique bond was shared language and shared tragedies. They held rotating parties every month and, until I was about 12, and old enough to babysit myself, my parents shlepped me to cramped apartments throughout the five boroughs where, as was European custom, children were segregated from adults. This meant I was shuttled to our host's kids' room while the adults drank so much vodka and schnapps that the men would burst into Polish and Yiddish folk songs, and soon the walls would vibrate as everyone joined in.

So it was in one such bedroom, behind a wall of foreign noises, that I recall being semi-annually assaulted by the pampered but excessively horny wrestle-maniac of a son of one set of friends, a boy just one year my senior and thankfully my own height. Whenever it was his mother's turn to host, I knew my fate was to spend the next couple of hours wrestling him incessantly on his bed until I had either completely subdued him (I always won) or my mother walked in, carrying my coat. She never seemed to notice that my hair was a mess, my clothes awry, and my face red with exertion. Secretly, I liked wrestling this kid and feeling his body tense beneath mine. I always took unfair advantage and hurt him more than I had to, not satisfied until he groaned in pain.

In another such bedroom, in another home, the far older son of another set of friends convinced me to let him rub my breasts and lie next to him while he kissed me. I liked him. He was handsome and gentle. But he was about 22 and I was about 11 so I knew there was something weird about it. From what I knew of his family, his politically zealous father, his schizophrenic mother, I mainly felt sorry for him, and whatever incredible loneliness led him to kiss me.

Most times the children of my parents' friends were reasonably normal and sweet on the surface but their boundaries were fractured and, like me, their inner lives fraught with terrors, phobias, depression and mystical beliefs. They confessed their sexual secrets, they showed me their porn collections, they touched me too affectionately, they confided things that I barely understood and, in the end, I'd go home with a headache and a gaping well of surprise in my soul. But affecting an earnest air while people spilled their madness came naturally to me and I couldn't help but encourage them and pat their arms as they spoke.

I remember only one older boy, by far the nicest of the lot, who treated me as one should treat a child. He treated me respectfully, showed me his airplane models and taught me to play Go because, he said, he thought I was unusually smart. I wished he was my brother and that I could live with him.

But in one Brooklyn bedroom, when I was about 10 or 11, lurked the unhappy 17-year-old son of some particularly messed up Survivors, and their problems seemed to be manifest in his flesh. He had a speech defect, a lazy eye, anorexia, and severe acne. Pustules surfaced as we spoke. I remained calm when he told me a dirty joke and snickered with him about sex. This emboldened him, and he decided he would be my guide to the world of adult sexuality.

He began by showing me his small collection of nudist magazines hidden in a drawer of his desk. They'd been handled so many times, the pages hung off the center staples like broken wings. He had to lay it flat so I could look at the pictures.

It was the first time I saw a naked adult male penis and I was stunned. Far from my expectation that a penis was a proportionate aspect of the male body, the guys in this magazine had dongs that dangled below their knees, and, in one alarming case, extended literally to the ground, where the head rested on a rock. I was flabbergasted. How in the world could they fit inside another human body?

"Is that real?" I whispered.

("Because," I said silently to myself, "if that's how all men are built I am NEVER having sex.")

"Look!" he held up a small tool that pushed a tiny rod into a hole when you pushed it on the bottom. "What do you think?" he murmured, staring at it raptly, his pus pimples glistening in the neon glow of his desk lamp. "Do you get it?"

"Get what?" I was so grossed out I went and sat on the bed. The giant penis freaked me out. It couldn't be real. To my exasperation, he dove beside me, grabbing my shoulders as he clumsily landed, and pinned me down under him. I wasn't afraid but I was really annoyed.

I was wearing a very stiff, uncomfortable and ill-fitting dress that my mother had bought for me. It had a stiff lining that itched like hell and made the skirt bell out. She also insisted I wear stockings for the party. My garter belt was a hand-me-down that had seen better days – days when, for example, the elastic still had elasticity, and the metal clasps did not leave claw marks in your thighs when you fell backwards.

Before I could dig the claw out of my leg, he'd managed to poke the tip of a finger under my panties and inside me.

"Do you like that?" he asked in an oily voice.

"Not really," I said.

A sudden surge of drunks desperately needing to piss lined up for the bathroom next door made us jolt upright, and I quickly rearranged my dress and bolted. I found my mother tipsy and smiling. She smoothed my hair. "Did you eat yet?" she asked. "There's a bird."

I never told anyone about my experiences. I preferred keeping them to myself so I could think about them later. Telling my parents was out of the question: no matter what happened, it was always going to be my fault in my mother's eyes, and would trigger a week of drama and screaming. When someone said something bad about me, my mother was always the first to agree. Keeping everything to myself was the only way to maintain my dignity.

Besides, furtive encounters never frightened me. They made a strange kind of sense. Being intimate didn't seem unnatural, and boys who wanted to touch my magic spot and give me pleasure hardly seemed like enemies, even though I knew they shouldn't be doing those things with me. I knew if I was their age, I would never ever do any of those things with a child. But I wasn't really a child, was I? In my desperate impatience to grow up, I resolved to act grown up and reject childish things. I knew that I could fake it until I was a real adult, and that's what I wanted.

There was one person, however, who really made me nervous. He was the mentally challenged caretaker at a Jewish center which hosted special events for Survivors. Everyone loved him and mocked him – loved him because he acted like a trained monkey when he was around them, and then, when his back was turned, smirked at his simple ways. He filled the familiar role of the village idiot, a reminder of everyone's slow cousin or that brother who "isn't quite right." He played the role of jolly fat boy with a heart of gold to the hilt. He did little favors for everyone and shunned tips.

To my mother, that made him the perfect free babysitter, and she sent me off with him to wander through the janitorial back-corridors of the building. He always fussed about checking the furnace, and made it our last stop every time. The furnace room was dungeon-like: pitch-black, warm, seemingly impenetrable. He would come up from behind and hug me, clasping his palms over my newly sprouted breasts as he did, and holding me tight that way for a few minutes.

He never did more than that. His touches didn't scare me either. But after a couple of visits to the furnace room, I wouldn't go with him anymore. I knew he must be crazy to treat a child that way. He was an adult. He was in his 30s or 40s. There were no built-in protections – no parents lingering outside the door. In fact, I wasn't sure if they could even hear me scream from the furnace room. Being alone with this man meant only one thing: under the right circumstances, he could turn into a Nazi.

And there it is, one of the saving graces of my youth. I never thought sex was bad but I always knew that people could be.

❧ Summer Camp Sex ☙

⌘

Istarted attending summer camp when I was eight years old. The first one was a day camp run by the YWHA, a long walk away from my parent's apartment in Borough Park. From there, we were shipped by yellow school buses to a park facility in Staten Island to do fuck-all all day. It was so phenomenally dull there and I felt so completely lost, my chief memory is of simply wandering around the edges like a shy dog off a leash, stopping now and then to be fascinated by something in nature. I watched bluebottles skim the pool for hours. I'd never seen dragonflies before. They looked like prehistoric flying monsters yet they were so beautiful and their color a brilliant blue I'd never seen. I ran shrieking whenever one flew near, moving to my next source of wonderment – another bug, a butterfly, a flower, a weed. Whatever was new captivated me.

But I do recall our one overnight camping experience, if only because I was awakened the next morning to hot humid breath blowing on my face.

A girl I'd talked to on the bus was mouth-breathing over me, only inches away.

To this day, nothing gives me the heebie-jeebies like being awakened to find someone's face covering my entire field of vision.

"What are you doing?!"

"You're so beautiful when you sleep," she said, "you look like an angel."

I pulled the blankets over my head until she left, and avoided going anywhere near her until camp season ended. It wasn't the first time another little kid had, out of the blue, worshipfully glommed onto me, and I hated it. What did they want from me? I knew they thought I knew more because I tried to act that way but I also knew I was a total fraud. I couldn't be whatever they wanted me to be. At that age, all my energy was devoted to trying to be what my mother wanted me to be.

Once my mother realized that no one criticized her for sending me away, and that, in fact, it made her look more middle class, she immediately looked into a sleep-away camp for me and signed me up for Surprise Lake Camp in Poughkeepsie, NY. Never mind that the camp was Zionist, while my parents embraced the diaspora; never mind that they made us say Hebrew prayers on Shabbos, while my parents were vehement atheists. The camp was Jewish and offered a generous subsidy for the children of the poor. So off I went to a truly strange new land among a breed of people I'd never known: American Jews.

American Jews and European Jews are such different kinds of Jews it deserves several volumes as a subject. We are the same and totally different, something like the difference V. S. Nailpaul talks about between Indians who were raised in India and those raised in Trinidad. You look alike; you use some of the same foreign terminology; you eat the same foods; but you are fundamentally as different as any two people from different worlds could be.

Everything about Surprise Lake boggled my mind. The kids seemed infinitely more assimilated than I'd ever be, with American attitudes and American arrogance and entitlement and a crudeness you didn't see among the well-mannered children of European Jews. In other ways, they were so much more Jewish than me – they knew all the prayers and rituals and holidays, things about which I was mainly ignorant. They came from "nice Jewish homes," and seemed rich to me – all the girls had new clothes, good haircuts, thick sweaters and fashionable socks. I looked like every other Brooklyn street urchin, in flimsy shorts and t-shirts from discount stores, with my father's sweater that shrank in the wash to keep me warm.

Also, for the first time in my life (or consciousness, really), boys and girls were completely segregated. Until then, I thought such Puritanism only happened at Catholic schools. One side of the lake was for girls; the other for boys; and between us was a very long gravel road. On Friday nights, teen campers would be allowed to attend a social on the girls' campus. I remember perching in the woods not far from the bungalow where they danced, watching the shadows of bodies doing "The Freddy," the dance craze that summer. We girls made chaperoned trips to the boy's side for events at the beautiful amphitheatre, named after its benefactor, the vaudeville star Eddie Cantor. I'd joined a camp theatre group and we were staging a production of *Bye Bye Birdie* so I got to go there a few extra times.

One of the reasons I'd first signed up with the theatre group was because two counselors I loved were involved in its production. They were the coolest couple I'd ever met. They were sweet, bohemian, and always acted glad to see me. Jean was tall and blonde and fair, with the palest blue eyes I'd ever seen; Jim looked 8 feet tall (probably closer to 6), with black hair and chestnut eyes and a white smile that came easy. He looked like a Jewish lumberjack and she looked like an Aryan sea goddess.

What I remember most, though, is the night we performed *Bye Bye Birdie*. It was one of the happiest nights of my childhood. I was filled with joy and hope about my future as a great star of stage and screen. Jean was calling and clapping at me, and Jim gave me a billion dollar smile to let me know I'd done good. I had just turned ten and I had never received that kind of praise at home. I was high as a kite on the goodness of life.

I was also only about half a year away from menstruating. The hormones were already in burbling turmoil inside my undeveloped body, though I didn't know it then.

All the kids were completely exhausted by the time the show and its after-events were finally over. I could barely keep my head up. I walked with Jean and Jim but after a few minutes, I was finding it hard to keep up. Someone, perhaps Jean, perhaps Jim, suggested that he should try to carry me the rest of the way back. He was, at first, more than willing and before I knew it, I was hoisted up into his powerful arms, raised to what felt like a towering height.

Where does sex begin? Where do sexual feelings begin? How to measure it? I was so young, I had no thought in any way, shape, or form that night of actually having sex with this man. I wouldn't kiss him or anything him! He was practically married to the most beautiful goddess who ever lived.

And yet...and yet...

Within moments of him lifting me into his arms, I woke up. Every part of me woke up. I was completely alive and awake and energetic. I loved being in his arms. I just loved it more than anything I'd ever loved before. I could feel his strong forearms wrapped tightly around me, cradling me gently, as he gallantly trudged forward with his increasingly heavy bundle. I suspect he was more interested in impressing his girlfriend but all I could think of was how I never wanted to leave his arms.

So when he noticed my eyes opening, and, later, that I didn't look half as tired as I should have, he would softly ask, "Do you think you can walk now? Are you awake?"

Each time, I would immediately shut my eyes and pretend to softly snore, as if whatever fit of consciousness he'd witnessed was some strange tic I had during my coma of sleep.

Jim must have been about 19 or 20, but to me at that time, he was all man. That poor, chivalrous, sweet boy carried me a mile in his arms until he laid me down in my bed, and he and Jean whispered their goodnights.

I felt guilty about my lie but it was my first awakening to an emotion that I had never before had. In that moment – as in many more moments yet to come – I could not, would not, let go of how good it felt to be in a man's arms.

What really made me ashamed, though, was that I loved making him suffer for my sake.

❧ The Girls of Summer ☙

⌘

Jean wasn't the first or only female who I perceived to be an image of womanly perfection. I was eager to make friendships. When I met a girl who seemed especially nice, I couldn't wait to spend time with her. I was curious about being female and what it meant to other girls. I looked up to older girls, especially the ones the boys liked most, and wished I could become as wonderful as they were. I noticed how one always wore her hair in beautiful styles, or how another had found just the right shade of lipstick for her complexion, or how another held her body differently when a sexy boy came near.

I never expected girls to be mean, though, and felt disappointed, even offended, when girls acted like jerks or ganged up against someone. As I learned my first summer away, girls could be positively evil in groups. They competed viciously, they gossiped cruelly, and their shots went straight to the heart. If you didn't play along, they short-sheeted your bed or stuck your fingers in warm water while you slept so you'd piss yourself. One summer, I was the object of a slew of pranks and, as much as it hurt, it hardened my heart to peer pressure and made me seek out better company.

Over time, I gravitated towards older girls and counselors. They were more understanding, less competitive, and more interested in talking about boys than tormenting other girls into conformity. They were gentle with me, aware of our age difference, and I got girl-crushes on them all, year after year.

There was Anya, the always tanned, highly intellectual daughter of a wealthy politician, who loaned me books about socialism, and protected me from some mean girls by taking me under her wing. There was Annabelle of the long curly hair and light blue eyes, a girl of rare and dreamy beauty. Wherever she sat, a cluster of boys soon formed. I thought they were all in love with her, just as I was in love with her. She was so beautiful I didn't have the nerve to approach her, fearful my presence would displease the glorious fairy princess.

My favorite was Claudia, an ethereal teenager with eyes as big as plates and an impossibly slim, perfect figure. Claudia was troubled like me, and restless like me, and intellectual too; but Claudia was beautiful and tall, and dressed in expensive blouses and adorable sandals and boots, and was rumored to be having affairs with all the best looking male counselors. Claudia followed crazy whims every day, and took too many drugs and was wildly unstable. She told me that she had to watch *Leave It to Beaver* every morning, because it helped her believe there was such a thing as a normal life.

As a lifelong night-owl, it was a joyful revelation that, at summer camp, you could hang out with other night-owls and yak the night away. At home, I'd lie awake and invent new things to worry about. Summer camp was the beginning of my abiding love of talking until dawn with a friend. I was enchanted when a girl named Lila cajoled me to hang out in bed with her. I was 10 and she was an older woman of 12. Lila positively overflowed with dirty jokes. I don't know if she got them from an older sibling or a relative, but her storehouse of bad jokes was impressive. We giggled so much, the girl in the bunk below complained. I was too young to understand most of them but I laughed anyway. But after the jokes, Lila thought we should kiss, and I wasn't sure about that. My best friend Ruby had recently begun kissing me whenever we were alone, and Lila's kisses were like hers: heavy and wet and scary in their intensity. I hopped from her bed. I didn't want anyone slobbering on me like that again.

Almost every year I attended sleep-away camp, I'd develop friendships that led to late-night, even all-night, conversations, sometimes curled up side by side in our pajamas, sometimes with sweaters on outside so we could look at the star-spangled skies.

The last time I shared a summer camp bed with a girl was in my last month of what turned out to be my last year of attending summer camp.

Carmen was an extremely intelligent girl, but introverted and mysterious. She was different from us: bigger, stronger, more masculine than the other girls. She was very polite, but solitary and seldom joined either our games or our conversations. That she had a wall up around her thicker than permafrost only made me feel empathy, because I sensed she must be wounded to act that way.

One night she called to me softly in the dark and invited me to talk. The other girls were sleeping but she must have heard my bedsprings creaking. I tiptoed over and slid in beside her. I was glad for the chance to get to know her. She mystified me. We weren't long into our conversation when she asked if she could tell me a secret. I had to promise I'd never tell anyone. I solemnly swore I never would and, until now, never did.

She needed to tell someone. Her father was having sex with her. Using her like a woman. The whole family knew. No one was making him stop. She couldn't stop him. She didn't know what to do. She needed to get it off her chest. It was making her crazy.

I didn't know what to say, much less how to help her or reassure her. How was it possible that a father could do this to a child? Obviously it was possible, just as the Nazis were possible.

I waited until she told me everything, until she exhausted her tears, until she calmed down. Then I went to my bed. I'd absorbed every molecule of her pain into my core until I couldn't absorb any more. A wall came down inside me and my stomach ached. I tried to block the images from my mind of Carmen's torment but I couldn't.

The next day, she acted like she barely knew me, and I reluctantly backed away, embarrassed by what I knew.

It was a relief knowing camp would be over in another week.

ॐ The Boys of Summer ☙

⌘

I was about six weeks short of my 11th birthday when I spotted Martin at the summer camp I went to the year after my immersion in American Jewry at Surprise Lake. It was the first time the sight of a boy made me freeze in my tracks.

The new camp was more my speed. It overflowed with immigrants and the children of Survivors. Camp Hemshekh, which means "the continuation" in Yiddish, was founded by Holocaust Survivors for their children. Politically, they were Bundists who promoted secular Judaism. For them, as for my family, being Jewish was about cultural heritage, not religion. Atheists welcome. While I was ignorant of Hebrew prayers, I spoke Yiddish and knew about Yiddish music, theatre and books from my father. There was no fuss about Shabbos at this camp, no religious ceremonies, no kosher food. Our common ground was the Holocaust, and the camp's goal was to keep secular Judaism and the Yiddish language alive. It made me happy to be at a place with a purpose and cause I could wholeheartedly endorse.

More important to me, though, was that the camp was filled with interesting weirdoes and non-conformists. There were hippies and folkies, and people who talked casually about sex and relationships. They seemed so enlightened compared to the children I knew back in Brooklyn, and a century ahead of the kids at Surprise Lake, who accepted chastity as their moral condition. Here, boys and girls freely commingled, walked arm in arm, and draped themselves on each other's laps. Hugging was allowed. The way some older girls kissed their boyfriends, you could tell they were having sex. It amazed me. I felt like I'd entered some kind of left-wing free love commune.

It looked like a place where you could love and be loved by a lot of people. That was a place I wanted to be. I could never love only one person for the rest of my life. It was not in my blood. I never had a time in my life when I loved only one boy. From the day I became conscious that boys were sexy, there were always at least two, or three, and often more, who I crushed on.

Even as I romanced my pain-suffering sweetheart Walter, I'd been secretly consumed with desire for the After School Center supervisor, a rail-thin young male teacher with jet black hair. I also had a love/hate relationship with the boy who'd asked me out on my first date, a strong, handsome boy named Luis Rivera. Meanwhile, I nurtured the fantasy that I would eventually have an affair with Spartacus, or at least his earthly incarnation, Kirk Douglas. Ever since seeing the actor tied nearly naked to a cross in that movie, I had been fantasizing about him obsessively at night. I didn't know how I'd ever get to meet him, I just knew it was in my destiny to tenderly wipe his brow and kiss his forehead while he twisted in agony.

Boys and men were everywhere, and while some were deeply annoying, others were strangely entertaining and a handful were phenomenally attractive and overwhelmingly magnetic. No matter what, they were almost never boring. It seemed only natural to get to know as many as possible. When my parents took me to see *The Sandpiper* around age ten, it proved to me that women could choose to love who they wished. That was who I wanted to be. I wanted to live the way free people lived. They never held back. They risked everything for the mere chance of ecstasy.

From the instant I laid eyes on Martin, I thought he was the Romeo to my Juliet. I trailed after him with puppy dog eyes, seizing every opportunity to sit beside him in dining hall or during the after-dinner counselors' break. Martin was a much older man, a sophisticated 16 to my starry-eyed 11. And while I wished he'd kiss me, he treated me like a little sister and tolerated my peskiness even when it interfered with him chatting up girls his own age.

The next summer, I was riper. Many more age-inappropriate touching episodes had occurred. I was developing breasts. My interest in boys was changing from indifferently friendly and aloof, to keenly observant and hungry for approval. My feelings for Martin were as steady as a rock. Again, I traipsed after him all summer, and our deep conversations about our lives and our future plans continued as if uninterrupted by the ten months of separation. He promised to take me to the Bronx Zoo and show me the yak, and I told him all my hopes and dreams.

The summer after that, I was a teenager. My obsession with Martin was now full-blown and dripping with lust. It had been another hectic year of erotic experiences for me, including that first French kiss with Marek. I was ready for love, I thought. I was ready for sex.

Oh, I was so young. I thought I was ready but Martin knew I was not. I remember he was hesitant when I snuck into his bunk one night and stole under his blanket. He was fully dressed, which surprised me. I climbed on top of him, gently winding my arms around his neck. I pouted my lips and he kissed them. I tasted stale, bitter tobacco on his lips. It turned me off, and then it totally turned me on. I kissed him harder and kissed him again and then suddenly felt his belt buckle sticking me through my jeans.

"Ouch, your buckle," I said, trying to shift.

"It's not my buckle," he said.

"What is it, then?"

There was a long pause before Martin said, in a kind voice, "You should go back to your bunk. You're really young."

Aborted though it was, the experience opened a door to sex for me that I couldn't wait to race through. And though I never did fuck Martin, he ended up introducing me to the first boy I did.

❧ Song of Solomon ❧

⌘

Martin didn't return to camp the next year, and while I missed him, I was always dreaming of the opportunities ahead, not the ones lost. I was 13, about to turn 14, and found myself suddenly being courted by a boy my age named Bobby. The courtship part must have been very brief, because all I remember is that we had a couple of happy evenings together kissing passionately in a dug-out behind the baseball field, where tall grasses hid us from the prying flashlight of the camp's administrator, a dour Holocaust Survivor who spent his evenings trying to pry amorous teenagers apart.

As for Bobby, I didn't know anything about him, except that he was a popular boy, was incredibly cute, with straight brown hair, bright red lips, a sharp nose, and a handsome beauty mark on one cheek. He gave me his ID bracelet, and I wore it proudly but didn't feel bad when he asked for it back at summer's end either. He was fun to kiss but we had nothing to talk about.

All summer, I restlessly pined for the boys and men I couldn't have. With Martin gone, my soul twisted for several smart, sexy older counselors, all of them out of my league. Many of them were boys who Claudia had mesmerized, and I'd lurk in their midst wishing I was beautiful and older and smarter and could be just like her.

They were nicer to me than kids my own age, so nice that I decided one afternoon that I wanted one of them to devirginize me. I waited until everyone was sleeping, and fled into the chilly Catskills night straight to the bunk of the boy who'd always been the kindest to me. I shook his arm until he stirred, then hopefully explained to him that I didn't see the point of virginity and would appreciate it if he would agree to help me get rid of it. It was preventing me from being an adult and I didn't want it anymore. As I talked, he propped himself up on one elbow, his eyes falling out of his head. When I was done, he told me he didn't think it was a good idea and urged me to go back to my bunk, smiling and patting my head the whole time.

No one wanted me. Even handsome Bobby was small consolation, since I'd felt no bond with him. I wanted something deep, something real. All around me, people were pairing up and breaking up and having secret liaisons, while my life was all in my head. During camp socials, I'd invariably wander outside to a patch of tall grasses to watch the stars, wishing someone might notice me and sit down to talk. Still, I felt better alone with my grasses and starry skies than indoors in a crowd of people who ignored me.

There was one secret source of happiness, a boy named Solomon. He was as odd as his old-fashioned Jewish name and had a dramatic flair I'd never seen in a boy before. It was a fanciful, rainbow-colored fashion period in general, but Solomon still managed to stand out. He wore high-necked Russian shirts and sometimes a dark cape which gave him a beauteously sinister air, especially when he moved quickly and the heavy fabric undulated like bat wings.

Although in public he had a beautiful blonde girlfriend with dark blue eyes and a goyishly snubbed nose, and I was a short, frizzy-haired, big-nosed nerd, he and I had many deep conversations in the recesses of the social center, and had come to an unspoken agreement that we both liked sex. This led to an invitation to visit his bed and make out with him, which I quickly accepted. It was really nice and he was very gentle. We only met a couple of times because I didn't feel good about the situation. For one, he had a girlfriend. For two, he treated me coldly in public so people wouldn't know how he really felt. And for three, his clutch of sidekicks who didn't know I was his girl on the side picked on me as an unwanted female intruder.

But in the fall everything changed. We were back now at separate schools, in different boroughs, far from the summer camp rumor mill, and when he called me, he said he missed me and wished it had worked out better between us. He was willing to travel all the way from the Bronx to my parents' house in Brooklyn just to see me. I was so happy, we immediately made plans.

A couple of weeks later, in my single bed in my old room in my parents' house in Borough Park, I removed all my clothes for the first time with a boy, and felt Solomon's soft lips brush the even softer lips between my legs. I didn't know what I was feeling, and it didn't feel like much, but I was amazed nonetheless that a boy would kiss me there. When he finished and sat up, I saw that a tiny piece of fluff from my jeans was stuck in his young beard. I wanted to laugh but I was still too amazed to speak.

He traveled back to see me a time or two again and finally invited me to return the favor, and visit with him. His parents would be away and we could spend as much time together as we wanted. At that age, that only meant "until dinner," but I planned it carefully, leaving early for school that day and immediately detouring to the subway to catch a train for the Bronx.

I remember his parents' apartment so clearly, its fine furniture and lofty air. His sunny bedroom was at the back and as soon as we got there, he said he wanted to shower, and told me it would be nice if I was naked when he returned. I undressed shyly, and sat waiting on the bed with a blanket draped around me.

He emerged from the bathroom still wet, and I thought a red rubber hand-shower was caught between his legs, with the end of it sticking out in front. But the tube kept moving and finally.... Oh! OHO! That was what a real penis looked like when it was erect! OHH!

And then a smaller "oh" because it was nothing like what I expected. I don't know what I expected. Until then, although I'd felt that hard male bump through underwear and jeans, I hadn't actually seen a naked erection. I had long ago concluded that the naked men in my acned suitor's nudist magazine were ridiculously fake, but I didn't realize a penis got so rigid or so brightly colored, like a giant vein springing from his loins. What a strange looking thing, I thought. It can't be comfortable.

Solomon brought me his penis. "Would you kiss it? Please kiss it."

He brushed it against my mouth. The skin was so soft! I kissed it.

"That's good, but open your lips a little, can you?"

Reluctantly, I opened them a smidge and gave him a wet kiss.

"Oh yes," he moaned, "again, please."

I covered the head with moist, plopping kisses. He looked at me hungrily, and I did the same to the shaft.

"Would you take it in your mouth? Please?"

"Mmmmm...." I looked him in the eye. "No."

"Let's kiss," he said. He dove into bed beside me and we began making out frantically.

"Put your knee in my groin," he said, "and rub it hard." He guided my knee to his balls. "Grind it in," he said.

"Are you sure?" I had always heard that boys' balls were so fragile that it hurt if you touched them.

He thrust his balls in my knee. "Don't worry, do it hard."

I began grinding my knee into his testicles and he kissed me even more passionately. "Harder," he whispered, "do it harder, harder."

I gave it my all. I had no idea boys liked that but it didn't bother me, so I kept going until my knee gave out. I don't know if he was satisfied. Neither of us had orgasms. But we stayed in bed, naked and making out, until twilight, when I had to make the long trip home to Brooklyn and dinner with a family who never had any idea how I lived my real life.

❧ The Emancipation ☙ of the Child

⌘

Nietzsche was wrong about "whatever doesn't kill you makes you stronger." World War II didn't kill my parents but it left them among the walking wounded, permanently weakened at the core of their beings, clinging to life like frightened animals.

My mother cultivated an atmosphere of insularity in the home, where everyone was expected to be afraid of the things she was afraid of. And since she was afraid of everything, every day was a minefield of anger and bitterness. Hiring a plumber, visiting a doctor – how did you know they weren't ripping you off? How did you know their work was good? My parents would curse and shout over the most mundane decisions for weeks. You never knew what would trigger their paranoia, and you never knew when the rage would come. You couldn't hold it against them, because they were Holocaust Survivors, but you couldn't let their damages control your life.

In my 14th year, my affair with Solomon now over, and my friendship with Martin at a new platonic depth, I spent one Saturday in spring with Martin and his friend Rory, a guy who seemed deep and serious, and was so phenomenally good looking, that I was dancing on air just to be out with them.

Look at me, I thought, on the town with two sexy grown men of 19!

We spent a long day together as a triad – visiting the Bronx Zoo, smoking dope at Rory's hippie crash pad, wandering out again to the Bronx botanical gardens. We walked and talked for eight hours, winding our way through unfamiliar streets.

When night finally came, Martin led us to another friend's place, and the boys ordered pizza for us to eat. It was late but I was starving so I decided to eat before heading home. At the last minute, I decided to call my mother to give her a heads-up.

"I want you here right now!" she shouted when I called. This surprised me. I explained that I was hungry and would get on the train as soon as I had dinner. My mother was usually panic-stricken that I would fall into starvation at any minute, and always urged me to eat more. Moreover, her interest in my whereabouts at any given time was, at best, whimsical. Usually I wouldn't call. I'd tiptoe in late at night and find her already sound asleep, waking up the next day to ask, "So when did you get in last night?"

"No! Leave this minute! THIS MINUTE!" she shrieked.

I walked the phone as far as I could, pulling the wire and the curly cord to their limits, so the boys couldn't hear. I whispered into the phone, "Is something wrong? What happened?"

"I'll tell you what's wrong, smarty-pants! You have no heart, you don't care what you do to your parents, do you know what you're doing to us?" I could hear my father fretting in the background as she whispered angrily at him to back off.

"All I'm doing is calling to say I'll be late," I said. "What's the big deal?"

"You're killing us!" she said. "How can you do this to your mother?"

I slammed down the phone before I could stop myself. I'd never hung up on her before. I was dazed by my own chutzpah.

I couldn't eat. My stomach was in knots. Martin and Rory and I rode the subway back to Sheepshead Bay in gloomy silence. When we finally got there, we saw my mother leaning over the porch railing and my father arguing with her. As soon as she spotted us, she began screaming so loud, lights went on in neighboring homes. My father grabbed her by the elbow and pulled her back inside before someone called the cops.

"Well, good luck," the boys said, looking embarrassed.

"You don't have to go in," Rory said. "Do you want us to wait?"

"No, no, I'll be fine," I shrugged. I was humiliated. I didn't want them to know how crazy my family really was. I knew something had probably gone wrong between my parents again and that it was the real culprit in my mother's rage. I couldn't let anyone see that. "Please go."

When I got inside, my mother followed me into my room, smacking me and screaming until she was hoarse. I was numb to her malice. Fuck her. This wasn't about me being late; this was about her need to punish and control. As long as I feared her rage, she would destroy me the way she'd destroyed my father. Let her beat me and scream at me all she liked. She would not control me again.

The next day, I found her standing at the window in my bedroom. Her shoulders sagged. She looked defeated, as tiny and forlorn as an abandoned child. She turned when she heard my footsteps. Her face was smeared with tears.

"I'm sorry," she said in a pitiful voice. "I don't know why I acted like that."

I didn't know what to say. It broke my heart to see her that way. I wanted to pick her up and hold her and comfort her like she was my child. I sensed it's what she wanted from me. I couldn't. I knew that her remorse would last only until the next time she attacked me, and that the only person she pitied was herself.

ஐ Into Life ⋈
and Out of Control

⌘

Until age 14, my pattern was to notice a boy and long after him until he noticed me (if he did at all), and then talk with him and get to know him as my longings budded and blossomed into kisses.

In my 14th year, though, everything changed when boys started noticing me before I noticed them. Now, instead of always watching from the sidelines until I picked out someone who seemed interesting and attractive, boys were approaching me before I had time to think about how I even felt.

With my family's move from our old neighborhood in Borough Park to our new home in Sheepshead Bay, the population changed from scattered, interracial groups of street urchins who played fierce sidewalk games and made out in janitorial hallways to a neighborhood of white middle class kids who sunned themselves with reflectors on front porches, played their stereos loudly and smoked pot, and whose friends drove up in sports cars. I resented being relocated to this pit of bourgeois entitlement at first but a few nights of inhaling salty air and seeing seagulls fly by my bedroom window quickly changed my mind. Inside the home, we were as poor as ever but to me it was like owning a summer place in walking distance from the sea.

Within a few days, I was yo-yoing back and forth from our new house to the Bay, and then from the house to the shopping district on Avenue U. Every day I'd pass homes where parties were in progress, seemingly all afternoon. The attendees were several years older than me, but sometimes they waved and acted friendly. I finally slowed my pace one day while shlepping groceries home and accepted a friendly boy's invitation to linger for a few on the porch. He and his friends were all nice looking guys in their late teens. While the first boy, Ken, was chatting with me, the others were obsessed with an insanely sexy girl who was there. She wore a nearly non-existent bikini, which showed off every inch of her tight curves, from her huge high breasts to a tiny waist and full hips. I was surprised when Ken told me I was welcome to come back and visit whenever I had the time. I looked like a rag-doll next to that beauty.

I took him up on the offer gratefully, and started spending my afternoons in their relaxed company. Ken was a very slim, fit, thoughtful preppy blonde boy of 19. He was more reserved than his friends, and seemed to have more spending money than them too. There was always food in his fridge and dope in his pipes. He had style and class unlike any boy I'd ever known. He had vacated his room in the main part of the house and moved into the basement, which he had turned into a kind of 24/7 party den for people he found interesting, a majority of whom were old school friends and friends or girlfriends of theirs.

Everyone's parents closed their eyes to what kids did together when they hung out. True, most of the time, it was the same things we did on the porch – listen to loud rock music, smoke a lot of marijuana, talk endlessly about the things we all planned to do when we escaped Brooklyn life and moved to Manhattan.

But, sometimes, there was sex. Sometimes, when I was alone with him, I gave Ken blowjobs, because he was really nice and now that I knew how to do it, it seemed like I should offer it to boys I really liked. Our intimacy was both relaxing and uneventful. It was friendly but in no way passionate. He was curiously calm during blowjobs. I never knew when he was ready to cum. It always happened suddenly, without him moaning or writhing or even seeming to be more than physically aroused. I found it really interesting and strangely cool that a person could be that cold in bed.

I remember once giving Ken a blowjob on his mother's beige living room carpet as we watched Iggy Pop go nuts on TV. First he destroyed himself on stage, then he threw his remains into the ravening arms of his roaring fans. Nothing changed in the temperature of Ken's passions though. As soon as he came, he started laughing about the rock star's wild performance.

Sometimes Ken screened porn in his basement – he specialized in the rare, the exotic, and the weird, seeking not only the one-of-a-kind but also anything of an adult nature that might shock his friends. So it was that I once watched a fuzzy grainy Danish 8mm movie showing congress between a woman and a horse. Ken had a sexually sadistic side, and had challenged his famously horny friend Hal that he couldn't come to a horse-fucking movie. Hal, ever eager to prove himself to Ken, and perpetually in the mood for an orgasm, asked to rest his head in my lap for the test. I was a little dubious but willing to go along with the bizarre game. So Hal lay back on the floor, head propped on my thighs, unzipped his pants and jerked himself off to orgasm while some Danish porn actress maneuvered with a horse.

Once I dropped in at Ken's and was surprised to find the inner door locked. When he opened it, he told me everyone inside was naked. They were having a whipped cream party. It was messy. Did I really want to come in? No, I really did not, I decided, so I left. Group sex sounded great theoretically but even removing my shirt with a man, at that stage, was extremely emotional for me, and something I only could do when I was completely alone with and really sweet on a boy. Plus whipped cream? No.

For me, Ken was an invaluable source of unusual information about sex. Once he lent me several issues of *Screw* magazine to peruse. I thought they were crudely funny and stored them in the bottom drawer of my desk for late night reading.

When my father picked me up at music school a few days later, he was unusually pale. I realized something was wrong when he began vaguely muttering and lecturing me on the ride home about how disappointed my mother was that a girl like me would... He never got to his point but by the time we drove up to the house, I knew I was in deep deep shit. When I got inside, crazy sounds were coming from my bedroom. I ran in to find my mother screaming curses in Polish. Spread across her lap was a now-infamous photo of Al Goldstein eating pussy with knife and fork, with a bottle of ketchup on the side.

"How could you?" she kept repeating. "To think a daughter of mine...." She sobbed. When she cursed, "Kurwa jego mać," I started to laugh. It literally translates as "your mother's a whore." But she started hitting me and it turned into another small family adventure, with my father trying to make her stop even as he defended her for doing it.

Fortunately or unfortunately, my mother never blamed my friends for anything. She always blamed me. So I merely returned the *Screw* magazines to Ken, and never disclosed the recent unpleasantness over their discovery.

Ken would come and go for almost 20 more years of my life, but his was not the only house on the block where my sex education progressed almost too fast for me to fathom.

ဆ Unlike Other Girls ಞ

⌘

U nlike other girls, I was never afraid of boys. I saw no real
tangible differences between boys and girls except in their
physical anatomy and their tendencies to pursue different in-
terests.

Unlike other girls, I wasn't ashamed to discuss sex or to freely
confide my exploits to my girlfriends. I was often the go-to girl
when it came to questions about how to avoid pregnancy and
how to improve one's sexual techniques. I remember my best
friends in tenth grade cornering me once and requesting that I
show them how to give a blow job. They were one and two
years older than me, but none of them understood what it involved. They handed me a banana with hopeful looks on their
faces, so I showed them how to kiss it and hold it and stroke it
to make a guy cum. My attitude about sex, practical and a little
giddy, made them laugh and relax.

By eleventh grade, I was detailing my sexploits in such graphic
detail to my lifelong friend Robin that she began constructing
my future autobiography with memorable phrases, such as,
"Wherever you go, you leave a trail of broken hearts and soggy
penises behind you." She helped me maintain a sense of humor about the things that happened to me and never blamed
me for my crazy choices.

I decided around this age that no matter what happened to
me, I would get through it. I was strong. I knew things other

kids didn't know. I understood more about life. As long as I didn't physically risk my life, I'd be okay because no one could emotionally unravel me. I could rise above it. I could handle the pain. I had walls inside me, and walls inside of those walls, that would protect me. No one could breach that final wall. I could think about the people who survived seeing their own babies burned alive. Nothing that bad would ever happen to me.

It was this sense of self, and confidence in my own sense of self-preservation, that made me eager to widen my social circles beyond the kids I knew from high school and to develop circles of older friends. It made me push boundaries with boys, even when I didn't want them for sex. I wanted to go further than anyone in my family had ever gone, I wanted to act out the radical social philosophy my parents preached but never practiced because they were too fearful to engage with anyone outside of their circles of fellow Survivors.

Not me. I suffocated in small circles. Life was full of opportunities for beautiful moments and interesting experiences. Why circle the same drain? From my extensive walking expeditions, I'd become really comfortable with the idea of constantly switching routes and exploring new ways to get wherever you wanted to go. That was life too. I didn't have to do the same things every day. I could explore something new every day if I wanted to. All I had to do was say yes to life when an opportunity to do new or different came along.

I was sitting on my parents' porch one afternoon when a familiar figure appeared. It was the incredibly cute woman who passed by every day at the same hour. I'd been admiring her for weeks. Her hair bobbed like a giant pouf of black cotton when she walked. She wore optimally stretched and faded jean cut-offs and a fresh white peasant blouse, with round horn-rimmed glasses propped on her button nose. We'd waved before but this time she slowed, and I leaned over the railing to talk with her.

She was Chloe from Coconut Grove, a place I'd never heard of but whose name instantly evoked images of white beaches and palm trees. Chloe was exotic fruit in our mundane neighborhood, with an angelic face and physical grace. She moved on suntanned feet like a cat and when she giggled, which she did a lot, her cheeks dimpled. She was 16 and a half, barely two years older than me, and lived with her boyfriend, Vaughn, just a few houses down from me. She was an emancipated teen. Chloe was living the dream!

I'd seen her boyfriend's clique. They never assembled on the front porch but instead hovered around the basement door. They were a shaggy assortment of seriously strange-looking oddballs and misfits, scruffy intellectuals in army surplus clothes with long hair and beards, often carrying jazz records or thick books under their elbows.

Vaughn was lurking on the sidewalk when I made my habitual trip to the grocery store the next day. He said hi in a soft tender voice, surprising from such a big beast of a man. Vaughn was over six feet tall and rock-star skinny, almost anorexic, and wore skin-tight jeans and a tight tie-dyed t-shirt. His head was enormous and a bush of tight frizzy wires sprang from his scalp, not soft and huggable like Chloe's but thick and angry like pubic hair. His face was monumentally homely – his lips were thick, his nose was huge, his eyes were muddy brown slits that stared out coldly beneath heavy lids. His skin was disfigured by years of acne that had created mountains and crevices beyond repair. But he talked like a perfect gentleman, educated and refined and clearly a brilliant guy.

At first, I was puzzled that so homely a man could have so gorgeous an angel as his girlfriend. It made me even more curious about him. It must have been his intelligence and, indeed, he told me he was in an advanced science program at a local college. He seemed light and friendly, a true warm-hearted hippie, and invited me sweetly to hang out, beckoning me to the basement door. I knew Chloe wasn't home yet, though, and felt uneasy about being alone with him, so I said I had to go to the store for my mother and would come by later that evening.

I pushed my food around on my plate that night, restless to find out about the beautiful Chloe and her mysterious boy-friend Vaughn. She had an enigmatic, soft sweetness that res-onated with me. There was darkness to Vaughn that both troubled and attracted me too. As soon as the dishes were washed, I ran out the door.

I was so excited about visiting them that the visit itself was a letdown. A couple of stoned hippies had a forgettable conver-sation, and Chloe passed out over a textbook. Vaughn studied me all night, finally sitting down close beside me on the couch, and prompting me to talk. When I left, he walked me out to the starry streets, kissed me lightly on the lips, and urged me to return. What he didn't know, and what I couldn't admit to my-self, was that I'd wished it was Chloe's lips I'd kissed that night.

❦ Chloe's Breasts ❧

⌘

By early summer 1970, Vaughn's basement became my most important escape from home, my favorite retreat, a place where something interesting was always going on and there was always someone deep and weird like me to talk to.

A crew of oddballs assembled there most evenings to listen to music together, smoke pot, and have rambling conversations about everything from the meaning of life to where they would score drugs. These kids were grubby compared to the sleek crowd at Ken's but also more intellectual, more serious, more ethnically diverse, and much better read. A lot of them seemed depressed, and some of them were manic dreamers, always coming up with plans and plots that the others quickly shot down. There was a philosophy major who was preparing to become a Zen monk and a college boy who idolized Mick Jagger. Everyone had big ambitions, everyone was broke, everyone (but me) did whatever drugs they could, and our religion was the music of John Coltrane.

An earth-shaking sexual revolution in my brain happened when I came across the collection of *Zap Comix* that Vaughn owned and traded with friends. He had a bunch of issues that have since become classics of underground comics. Though I read through them all, Gilbert Shelton, S. Clay Wilson and Rodriguez, it was R. Crumb's art that completely bent my mind. It wasn't just that the stories and characters were all deeply depraved beyond all reckoning. Even at that tender age I understood satire and knew that artists used grotesquerie to embody truths. It was Crumb's total lack of shame about sex. Until then, I thought my fantasies were extreme. Crumb's fantasies were both unfathomable and unfathomably hilarious.

Crumb was completely and totally unafraid to talk about sex, and the sicker it was the funnier he made it. His work was drenched with the terror and anxiety and freakishness and criminality of sex, and went to places no one to this day ever fully discusses out loud. His cartoons of a happy average American family having incest; of a girl my age sucking off older men until she turns into an angry feminist; of women with asses so high they were climbing up their shoulders and men with tiny, vacuous heads, it was all so brutal, so real, and nothing I had ever read until then had ever flooded my entire brain with thoughts and emotions like R. Crumb. It's like my entire adolescence morphed under the power of his comics.

Crumb was also a refuge from Vaughn's unpredictable moods. I knew that his homeliness depressed and angered him, he'd confided as much to me; I knew he was restless and deeply bored living in Brooklyn; and I knew he took heroin. The combination kept me on my guard. Though I was an avid pot-smoker, I disliked other drugs, including alcohol, which I thought the most degrading of all. After being a trip-guide a few times, I decided tripping was out of the question for me. I couldn't be out of control. I liked taking care of other people but there was no one I trusted to take care of me. So despite Vaughn's frequent goading, I refused his smack, his speed, his acid, his booze, and the other drugs he wanted me to do with him.

Vaughn didn't play pranks on people or instigate sexual mischief for fun, like Ken did. On the other hand, Ken's friends didn't resent him, even when he made them look like fools, because he had a talent for making it seem like good clean fun. Vaughn ruled by shaming people. He tested them and sneered at them if they failed. He was generous one day, then made you regret accepting his hospitality the next day. Every now and again, one of Vaughn's victims would rise up in anger for a few brief moments, only to sink back into sullen stonedness, knowing that, really, there was no better place to go for the thrills we all sought. He seldom turned it on me, though or if he did, I managed to rebuff him enough to avoid confrontations. I wasn't as aware of the dysfunction then as I am now, but I knew something was off.

Chloe was helpless in his grip. She belonged to him like a slave, only they never named their dynamic. He controlled everything. He made her go back to finish up her high school degree. He reviewed her homework. He chose their meals. He bought their drugs. For all I know, he even bought her clothes. When they were together, she nearly vanished, becoming only a pretty little shadow hovering in his dynamic background. She held a protected status as the one woman no one could flirt with, which kept her a little isolated from the crew.

Vaughn was sexually voracious and had no shame about it. He slowly began cajoling me into sex, as he cajoled many of the people, male and female, who partook of his hospitality. He never risked outright rejection, just continually acted seductively with me, trying to grind me down. That kind of pressure always meets resistance from me. Though Vaughn was very smart, it was Chloe who appealed to me. She was like another species from our down-at-the-heels hippie mob. She seemed fresher and cleaner and softer and sweeter and, most of all, she seemed genuinely happy. Next to her, and despite his intellect and social power, Vaughn was a dark wet mess.

After a few weeks of unsuccessful seduction, Vaughn finally figured out my weak spot. He invited me over one afternoon, and when I arrived, he welcomed me inside like a long lost relative. He ushered me into the cramped space and swept his arm dramatically towards the bed. Sprawled out in the nude, her soft belly and breasts as tan as her feet, was Chloe. Her breasts awed me. They were like inverted champagne glasses topped by big, dark-cherry nipples. Her dark bush was so silky and thick, it looked like fur draped between her thighs.

"Come have sex with us," Vaughn said, steering me to the bed. He dove beside Chloe and they looked up at me, urging me to join them. I sank down to the mattress awkwardly. This was new. I didn't know what to make of it. It didn't feel wrong but it didn't feel right.

"I can't," I finally said. I don't know what I meant by that, exactly, I just knew that the thought of taking off all my clothes with them horrified me. Despite having oral sex with several boys by then, I was still a virgin. I thought I looked hideous in the nude. I was most comfortable keeping my own clothes on while playing with a naked boy. This situation was too new for me to know what to do. "I really can't," I said.

"You don't have to have sex, just be with us," Vaughn said. "It's ok."

"Yes, just be with us," Chloe repeated, reaching out to me. "I want you here." I went into her arms and touched her soft naked skin. "Will you?" asked Chloe.

"What do you want me to do?" I asked.

"Just be with us," they said, and Chloe kissed me. I shyly rubbed her breasts, and kissed her shoulder. Vaughn had stripped off his shirt and unzipped his pants. They began kissing, keeping their arms around me.

"Put Vaughn's cock in me," Chloe whispered later.

I put my hand on his swollen cock and he moved and she moved until they were positioned right, and Chloe added her hand to help me guide his dick into her thick wet bush. Once the head was inside, I sat back and watched it vanish into her as they both moaned and began fucking hard, forgetting about me.

I had never seen people fuck in the flesh. Vaughn was sexy and intense, purposeful and sensual at the same time, writhing on top of her like a demon while she cursed and groaned beneath, lost in a sea of desire. It didn't turn me on. It fascinated me.

I held my breath when they came, and as soon as they slumped into exhaustion, I fled.

⁊ To Nirvana and Back ⳗ
Via the Bronx Expressway

⌘

The rest of the summer of 1970 was a crazy blur of crazy, so eventful I can't even parse it out in my head. As neglectful as my mother had been in the old neighborhood, in the new one she nearly completely signed out. I was on my own most of the time, with virtually no governance, just the usual stack of weekly chores, the mandate to be there when my father came home for dinner, and flexible curfews at night. If not for my father always wondering where I was, she wouldn't have kept tabs on me at all.

I usually got back from Vaughn's or Ken's basements after midnight. I remember walking the short distance home along Bedford Avenue under the eerie glow of streetlamps, everything so tidy and prim, you'd never guess at the goings-on behind the safe brick walls. Sometimes, I'd join my mother in front of the TV, where she stayed up late for Johnny Carson every night.

I was seeing a lot of Jan and Jamie, my best friends from Erasmus Hall High School, which I was still attending when we moved to Sheepshead Bay in the spring of 1970. Jan and Jamie were the girls who asked me to demonstrate a blowjob on a banana. During the school year, we smoked pot together every lunch hour in some remote outdoor alcove of the massive high school. Sometimes we cut class to get high. Jan always brought an orange, and – thanks to a generous older brother – often provided the smoke as well. Sometimes it was a tiny chunk of hashish, sometimes a joint's worth of pot, and a couple of times that rarest and sweetest of highs, keef, the golden pollen of the male hemp plant.

Once in a while we had to pool lunch money to buy a nickel bag but it was worth it. The three of us knew we were renegades and hippies, destined for very different lives, far away from Brooklyn. Our common ground was thirst for experience that was different from the lives we all led at home. We didn't believe in wearing make-up or dresses, we didn't believe in authority, and we were deeply wistful for a way out.

Our bond was intense, especially after going through the turmoil caused by the Kent State Massacre that spring. There had been riots and protests on campuses throughout Brooklyn. We got embroiled in a verbal altercation with the Tactical Police Force outside the front gate of Erasmus, and I broke my pinky when a crowd surge threw me forward against the gate. For years after, I liked to say that I gave my pinky to the Revolution but, really, I was just a klutz who got pushed by a panicky mob.

As cops herded us forward with tear gas and batons, I got sucked into the mob and lost sight of Jan and Jamie. I ended up hiking all the way to Brooklyn College and collapsed on the grass just in time to watch Abby Hoffman deliver a speech on the steps of the Administration building which students had occupied. The world was changing before our eyes, social justice would prevail, and all the old rules would soon be dead and gone. I felt part of the change. I was growing up in a thousand ways.

When Jan's parents went away to their summer place, she invited me and Jamie to move in for a week. It was easy to convince my mother to let me vanish for a week. I just lied and said Jan's mother would be there. It was the best week of my adolescence. We started our days in the evening, listening to Jefferson Airplane, smoking dope, talking until dawn. Jan's handsome drug-dealing brother came and went, and one night carved a huge chunk of hash off a brick he carried in his pocket and handed it to us.

I loved waking up in Jan's quiet brownstone on a tree-lined street near Prospect Park, all of us stumbling into the kitchen in t-shirts and underwear and starting the day with a joint. We had no money for food, so we emptied the family freezer, broiling steaks and lamb chops for every meal. Sometimes, we went to Manhattan. I loved riding the D train during rush hour in the opposite direction from everyone else, knowing that while the day was ending for office and factory workers, mine had just begun. We went to free concerts in Central Park, we wandered Greenwich Village poster shops, we did anything and everything that was free, and we'd head home in the middle of the night, tired and happy.

Life felt glum when that week ended. It was difficult for the three of us to get together now that I lived so far. So a few weeks later, Jan came up with a brilliant idea. The three of us, plus one more girl, Helen, would hitchhike to Cape Cod for a week. Jan had consulted a map, estimated the time it would take, and knew we could get there in one day. I'd been to the Cape a few times on family vacations, so it seemed like familiar territory. I was scared of hitching rides, but decided that doing it as a group probably made it safe. So, I told my mother I was going back to stay at Jan's place for another week, packed a knapsack and took the subway to the Church Avenue stop in Brooklyn, where my friends waited for me.

Jan's plan was simple: take the subway as far as we could, and then walk to the Bronx Expressway and stick our thumbs out for a ride. We'd go as far as we could get and then we'd find a place to sleep outside. It scared the shit out of me when I realized how risky the plan was, but I felt I'd come too far now to turn back. We stood by the side of the expressway, three fifteen-year-olds and one fourteen-year-old, in shabby jeans and t-shirts, and within no time at all, a man in a rusty 50s behemoth with fins pulled over and we jumped inside. Though I was quivering inside the entire time, nothing bad happened, not with that first guy who picked us up nor with any of the others who gave us lifts along the way without question.

I was feeling very buoyant by the time we got the last ride into our destination town, Hyannis. We'd jumped onto a pickup with a bunch of fishermen who had boats docked there. They were a jovial, weather-beaten, working class group of men, and I was having fun joking with them. My friends felt differently. The only kind of guys they liked were hippies, and these guys were straight. When one of the fishermen offered to let us sleep on his boat for the night, my friends shot the idea down.

They dropped us at the town beach, where Jan and Jamie found a free picnic table and grill and started preparing brown rice for our dinner. I was beginning to regret making this trip and sat alone on a bench to think. Helen wandered away and we lost sight of her for an hour. Just as the rice was finally done, Helen re-appeared with a surprisingly nice-looking, long-haired boy in tow. He told us that he knew a place where we could stay. It was all hippies. It was an island of hippies. It was really cool. He couldn't tell us where it was but he could show us. He would take us there if we wanted. Did we want? I didn't think it was a good idea, but my friends disagreed. He was carrying a motorcycle helmet and he didn't look like he'd eaten in a while. The girls filled a bowl of rice for him promptly and sealed the deal.

With only the name of a town, and a landmark to find, we got back on the road and slowly hitched our way. I remember getting into a rainbow-colored converted VW bus that was home to the hippies who were driving it. It was missing a door, but the driver kept passing his pipe back to us, so that made it okay. They drove us all the way, letting us off in a desolate town. Helen's friend told us to meet him by the church so we walked to the first church we saw and plopped down on its steps.

We waited. We waited. The streets were deserted. We smoked a joint. What if there was another church? Two of us formed a search party and returned. Nope, this was the only church. We sat on our bags and fidgeted. We walked into the middle of the street, peering both ways. The church bells rang at midnight. A few moments later, a motorcycle rumbled up to us. It was the boy from the beach. He would take us one at a time, but the trip wasn't very long. I hadn't fully grasped that he was a biker until then. I could not believe we were placing our lives in the hands of a man in a black leather jacket. What if he was taking us to a biker bar for a gang rape? But the girls were excited and one after another vanished on the back of his bike. When he returned for me, I saw no way out of it. There was no other direction but forward. I grabbed his jacket tight and off we went.

He was right, it wasn't a long ride. We drove down to a sandy patch of beach, and my girlfriends were waiting at the shore.

"We're going to that island," he said, pointing to a dark shape in the distance. "We'll borrow a rowboat, it'll be okay, get in," he said, helping my girlfriends aboard.

I stood back on the shore. "Borrow? Do you mean STEAL?"

"It isn't stealing," he said, "I'll bring it back tomorrow."

Oh the logic. I stood on the shore fretting. It looked much too small to carry five people out to the island. What if the owner reported us to the police?

"We're going," they chorused from the boat, "are you going to stay there all night?"

I climbed in, half-expecting cops to jump out of the bushes. But we rowed off without misadventure. About halfway across the water, the rowboat sprang a leak. We bailed out water as best we could with our hands and hats. I was beside myself. *Of course*, I thought, *of course it has a leak*. I was on a stolen boat in the middle of the night crossing an unknown body of water to an unknown island a couple of miles from a town whose name I'd already forgotten, and now we were sinking. I tried to resign myself to death by stupidity.

When we pulled closer to shore, I heard and then saw pale monkeys shrieking in the trees. One screeched out our guide's name.

"Hehehe," he explained, "they dropped a lot of acid tonight, they're fucking around in the trees." He looked up again. "They're naked. I don't know what they're doing up there."

He moored us and we jumped out. I can't describe the catharsis of discovering we had lived through our journey and come to a place where hippies were tripping. It felt so safe compared to everything else.

We spent several days there – the number of days has faded along with some of the memories. But some details are as vivid now as they were then.

Three hippie brothers were caretakers for the island and had turned it into an anarchist commune by inviting fellow freaks to visit throughout the summer. Clothing was optional. Pot was in abundance. They carried fresh eggs and produce to the house every day. Outside, musicians jammed and women wove. The hard working brothers cleared land and took care of the farm animals, blistered their skin in the sun and returned in the evening with bruised and calloused hands. It was a universe of natural living and drug orgies contained within this perfect floating oasis.

I was a little sad when my friends went skinny dipping with the others. I still could not remove my shirt for more than one person at a time. I sat away from them, watching enviously, when the eldest brother, Jake, sat down beside me. The sun was setting. We were drenched with red light and glowing together. He said he noticed me because I always seemed to be alone, thinking. He liked that I was solitary, he said.

He took me inside and then cooked a simple dinner of fried eggs and bread, called for his brothers to join us, and had me eat at the kitchen table with the three of them as if I was family. His brothers kept smiling but said nothing the whole meal. That night he told me to sleep with him in his bed, instead of on the floor, but to keep my clothes on. I guess he was a good Catholic. He held me gently all night but didn't kiss me or touch me anywhere. Jake fell for me so fast it surprised me. He was sweet too, though I didn't feel anything for him beyond gratitude and friendship. By the second day, he was suggesting that I stay with him for the summer.

I remember standing outside the main house, watching everyone in motion, and wondering if this was the moment for me to change my life. I didn't have to go home. I could find a place for myself here. Maybe this was where I belonged, with laid-back, nature-loving hippies on an island off the coast of Massachusetts. I wished, I wished so hard, I could feel desire for Jake or love or some kind of spark at all, but I didn't. Plus I was starting eleventh grade in the fall. I wanted to go to college.

And yet. I had been dying to run away from home since I was ten. There were times I wanted it so badly I felt I'd rather die than live at home another day. And yet. Could I? Live with a boy I didn't know or desire to escape my life?

Jan and Jamie made the decision I couldn't. After a few days, they felt restless. I tried to talk them into staying longer but they were set, so I reluctantly agreed to leave with them. Jake was hurt but, noble to the end, ensured we had a sound vessel for our return to the mainland and, even better, a safe ride for part of the way. Before we knew it we were back on the road, in a van with two silent boys who dropped us off on a highway.

A couple of days in Jake's company had made me more sober. My friends chattered obliviously while I stewed. Why did we leave such a gorgeous place? We had no place better to go. In fact, we didn't have a destination now at all. They just wanted to rove. I didn't understand why they wanted to leave the shelter of paradise for the dreary uncertainty of the road. It was a stormy day, then a hungry night, stranded in the rain and fog with no cars in sight. It didn't have to be like this, I steamed. We didn't have to be standing in the pouring rain hoping that someone would stop and take four teenagers for a ride to nowhere in particular. Who would even stop on a night like this?

A man whose radio blared out a hellfire sermon was the answer. He had glowing psycho eyes and was dressed like an undertaker. My friends hopped right in. It was the first car we'd seen in nearly an hour. They squeezed into the back and everyone agreed I should sit up front beside him.

He wanted to talk. A lot. First, he talked about sin and going to Hell. He told me to flip open the glove compartment. He kept a Holy Bible and a loaded .45 in it. He took out the gun and put it on the seat between us. He told me about the Coming of Jesus and how the Jews had killed him. I hoped he didn't realize I was a Jew. I wore my best, most respectful "how to act with parents" mask, didn't argue with his insanity or express my own opinions, and finally, with some lies and manipulations, managed to get him to let us off someplace safe.

This is where my objectives varied from my friends: they wanted him to take us somewhere. I just wanted to get us the hell away from him.

Maybe it was that glimpse of nirvana, the beautiful island inhabited by three loving brothers, which gave me an understanding that people can have happy lives, they can find a place of peace and a sense of purpose. Or maybe it was residual terror from the loaded gun glinting by my thigh. Whichever. I was done.

The next morning, I asked our first hitch to drop me off at the closest Greyhound station, over my friends' dismayed protests. It was hard to deal with their disappointment, especially when they helped me scrape together the fare and hugged me with sad faces. I felt like a traitor and a weakling for giving up. When the bus pulled out, I saw them lined up with thumbs extended on the sidewalk, and I dipped down in the seat, ashamed. But as soon as we were out of view, I popped back up, reveling in the cozy, air-conditioned double-seat I had all to myself. There were only a few passengers on board for the nine-hour drive to New York. No one even looked at each other. It was perfect. I sank into the unfurling time warp that is a long bus trip, happy in the quiet middle space between adventure and home, staring out the window and scribbling poetry all the way.

✧ If Thine Right Eye ✧
Offend Thee

⌘

These days, I think of 1970 as the year of Stonewall, the year that a small riot in a Greenwich Village bar changed the world.

But back then on Bedford Avenue in Sheepshead Bay, Brooklyn, this teenager was obsessed with her fantasies and dreams, and felt that nothing in life was more pressing than her personal sexual evolution from girl to woman.

These days, I can look back at her and shake my head at the hormonal storm that gripped that girl's brain. But in 1970, there was no standing back and analyzing what was happening to me. I was DRENCHED with confusing, conflicted needs and couldn't stop catastrophizing about them. I wanted so bad to be a woman, but I didn't want to do any of the things women did.

As my 15th birthday loomed, I brooded fitfully about my virginity. It marked me as a child. It felt shameful to be so sexually liberated and yet so desperately shy about that part of my body. I had to face it: as long as my hymen was intact, I couldn't have "real" love affairs. Grown men didn't take me seriously. How could they? I didn't go all the way, like real women. Consummation was the point of love in all the novels I'd read. How could I have great love without consummation? I was ready to join the ranks of adults. I had to stop being a virgin. I just had to. I had to find someone and do it and get it over with. Then I'd be a grown-up and ready for true love.

I hadn't seen Martin all summer, since last spring's humiliating episode when my mother took her Blanche Dubois act to the front porch, so I called him up. I laid out my case for why I needed to lose my virginity that summer. He was reluctantly sympathetic. He still had mixed feelings about being intimate with someone he knew as a child. But he did know someone I might really like. We arranged for him to visit me with his friend Amos, a boy I only knew by sight, as the long-term boyfriend of a really cool, artsy girl.

Everyone respected Amos for his intelligence. Now that he was an ex-boyfriend, he seemed like a good prospect for the devirginizing project. On his end, Martin had confided in Amos that I wanted to meet someone who would agree to be my "first." Amos was sufficiently intrigued by the strangely intense teenage girl who wanted to dispense with her virginity post haste that he agreed to meet me and see if we hit it off.

Once again, Martin brought acid, and once again, I was the sober tour guide. We wandered along quiet streets to the congested blur of seafood restaurants and clam bars on Emmons Avenue, and then across the sparkling waters of the bay by footbridge.

Amos was 20 years old. He seemed mysterious, dreamy and inward, different from the kind of boy I usually went for. Plus he'd been in a sexual relationship for a few years. That made him sophisticated and more attuned to females, I thought. Amos and Martin had long conversations about their college courses and subjects I didn't understand. This impressed the shit out of me. So did Amos' wavy blonde hair and porcelain complexion, pale blue eyes and long thin nose. He was so out of my league, it was hard to believe he was interested in devirginizing me. I was ecstatic.

After they went home, I waited by the phone. A week went by as I played and replayed the possibility in my head, wondering if he would ever call. Finally, the call came. I was invited to his place. Could I get to the subway station near his house? He'd wait for me, and walk me back to his apartment.

I spent the long subway trip there daydreaming and fuguing from reality, my brain swimming in crazy oceans of emotions. I wanted it. I didn't. I wanted him. I didn't even know him. I was doing the right thing. Was it the right thing?

It seemed like only a few minutes had passed when I ran up the subway steps to throw myself into Amos' friendly embrace. When we finally got back to his apartment, a small group of friends were partying in the living room. We joined them, and chatted for a while but then Amos pulled me away to his bedroom. A few minutes later, I heard the front door close as his friends snuck out, and then we were all alone.

Sun poured into the bedroom where I waited for my life to change. I didn't know how I felt. It felt surreal. I was going to be a woman, yeah! It was incredible. At the same time, it felt so banal, like nothing was really happening, just me on another bed with another boy on a sunny day, about to do something that billions of people had done before and millions were probably doing right that minute.

Amos stripped off his clothes and bounded to the bed. In a flash, I had a sense that it wasn't going to work. Now that he was kissing me, the chemistry felt off. His skin was too soft. He didn't smell right. I didn't feel anything for him. I closed my eyes. He began to kiss me between my legs. I didn't want him there. He was too aggressive. I suggested we get right to the main event, and he was game.

He got on top of me, positioned the head of his cock between my legs and gently pushed. Nothing happened. He pushed again. Nothing. He wasn't going in. It was like I didn't have a hole there or something. He pushed hard.

"Ow!" The pain was unexpected. "Does it have to hurt?"

"I can't get it in," he said, flustered.

He tried another angle and maybe got a bit of the head in. Maybe.

"This really hurts," I said. I was mortified. The pain was awful. Was my hymen made of steel?

"Well, you're a virgin, I guess you're tight. My girlfriend was always wet. I never had a problem getting in."

He pushed. He pushed. He got the tip in. He pushed more. Beneath him, I writhed in excruciating pain, biting my lip so I wouldn't shriek.

"Are you sure you're in the right place?" I gasped. "Is it in yet? Is it in?"

"No, no," he'd say. "Do you want me to stop?"

"No," I'd say, "don't stop. Owwww."

As bad as it was, my mind was made up. There was no point stopping now – it would hurt just as bad with someone else. I had to hang in: the hymen would break and I'd be free of it permanently. With every thrust it felt like someone was cutting me open. Meanwhile, his cock was getting sore.

"I don't understand, this never happened with my girlfriend," he said.

I looked up at him helplessly. Maybe something was wrong with me. Suddenly it seemed as if I'd always known that I was broken. I wanted to run all the way back to Brooklyn and hide in my bed for the rest of my life. I was broken, my pussy was broken, it was hopeless, he'd never get inside. I was naked and humiliated, and this man looked genuinely sad, and it wasn't his fault. I'd seen how easy it was for Vaughn and Chloe. The fault was mine.

"Let's try again," I said.

And so we did. And it happened all over again. No matter how or where he pushed, it was like trying to shove a kielbasa into a clenched fist.

I was on the verge of giving up when I felt him squeeze in a little further and start to pant.

"Wait," he said, sweat pouring down his forehead onto my face, gluing his long hair on my cheeks

"What?" I whispered.

"God!" he said. He collapsed on top of me.

"Is it over?" I asked, spitting out his long hair which had become trapped in my mouth.

"Yes," he sighed, rolling off. "I got almost all the way in."

"I'm getting dressed," I said, jumping off the bed. I quickly pulled my clothes on and waited while he did the same. We faced each other awkwardly.

"You ok?"

"Yes," I lied.

"Let's get something to eat. I'll take you to the diner," he said. "OK?"

"Sure." Anyplace away from that bedroom sounded good to me.

We went to the Riverdale Diner. Waiters dodged customers as they ran with heavy trays, families sat at tables eating meals, everyone was going on with their daily lives as usual. But inside me, every molecule, from brain to thigh, was kaleidoscoping. I wanted to scream out that I wasn't a virgin anymore but instead quietly followed Amos to a table. I could barely sit on the cushioned seat, my crotch burned so much. I excused myself and went to the bathroom to collect my thoughts.

When I pulled down my jeans, I saw it: a glob of gooey blood soiled my panties. It had really happened. I wasn't a virgin anymore. I was a grown woman now.

Or was I? I could never go through that crazy bullshit again. Fucking was *horrible.*

By the time I returned, Amos had ordered us hot deli sandwiches and the food was waiting. The piled-high pink folds of thinly sliced pastrami glistened and steamed like another woman's vagina.

"Are you ok?" he asked.

"I'm fine," I said.

I picked at the food on my plate, and waited until he finished.

"I need to get home now," I lied. There was still time but I couldn't face him. He'd seen the truth about me. I was an unlovable weirdo. Amos dropped me at the subway. The ride home took forever. There were no daydreams this time.

One more secret to lock away about myself, I thought. I failed at the most important sex act there was. I'd asked for that knowledge. I brought it on myself. I could've stopped him at any time but I refused. I was a stubborn idiot. But at least it was done. I achieved my tactical goal. I could call myself a woman. Whoopee fuck.

❧ Jack the Creeper ❧

⌘

Iwas restless all August and into September, waiting for school to begin. I wasn't visiting friends as much, still troubled by my experience with Amos. I wanted to be alone.

I spent my days exploring Sheepshead Bay. In Borough Park, I was always worried that if I went too far in certain directions I'd be walking into mugger territory. But now I could walk for miles feeling safe. I dawdled and meandered, scrutinizing store displays up and down Avenue U. I went into every one that looked even vaguely interesting, rationalizing that almost anything could be useful SOME day.

In the intoxicating leather smell of the luggage store, I pretended that I was buying bags for trips to Paris and Rome. In antiseptic smelling drugstores I'd sidle up nervously to ogle braces and ace bandages, incontinence equipment and other medical aids, fodder for that night's sexual fantasies. I'd linger outside the Avenue U movie theatre, reading the posters and lobby cards like books. I'd dip into an old-style Brooklyn bank that smelled of polished wood and oiled bronze and steal pink deposit slips with a thrilling sense of guilt. I'd get a slice of pizza and sit with it as long as possible, watching customers come and go and making mental notes of everything they said and did. Every day was an adventure, every adventure taught me something new.

My favorite stop was a women's jeans store. The owner was a Vietnam War veteran named Sal who'd come home with a drug habit and a new outlook on life. In a nutshell: live fast, die young. Sal didn't do anything slow. Sal dressed and acted like a hippie, with long, greasy brown hair and uber-tight bellbottoms and an anti-war, fight-the-power rap, but he was – in the parlance of the day – one uptight cat, folding and refolding jeans, unable to complete a thought if the seams didn't sit straight. He acted grateful to have company, shared cigarettes and joints freely, and we had long conversations at first, me sitting in his folding beach chair while he held court behind a tiny desk. He was the archetypal nice Brooklyn boy, but something was screwy. He talked continuously, like he was reading lines off a scroll in his head.

The more he yammered and twitched, the more nervous he made me. I didn't know what he was on but worried it was smack and speed that made him so wired. That double-scared me. No one could keep going like that. He was risking his life and maybe even mine if I kept sticking around. I didn't want to be there when he blew.

Once, Sal showed me an army souvenir. It was a snapshot from Vietnam. He wore a crew-cut and a uniform, and posed with some other GIs as if they were hunters, rifle butts resting on a dead enemy soldier. He wanted my reaction but I didn't know how to react. I swallowed my horror. I felt sorry for Sal, deeply sorry about what he had been through, sorry for his victim, sorry about war, sorry about people, sorry about life.

I cut back on visits to Sal. It was too much like being with my parents' friends. They acted friendly on the surface but in private they were all wounded, broken, angry. You never knew when they'd erupt. Their entire emotional context was predicated on fear. I wanted easy friends, people who didn't have deep problems. Sal was too scary.

I was heading back from a particularly unnerving visit with Sal when I passed a house where I'd often seen a man sitting in the yard. He looked like a fashion model. He seemed to be in his late 20s and was very lean and very blonde. He was soaking up the rays when I spotted him and, as had become our habit, we waved to each other. This time he got up from his chair, and walked to the hedge separating the sidewalk from his yard.

He had an amazingly white smile, as wide and sunny as a happy child's. He wore a light blue work shirt that matched the color of his eyes, and his cuffs were rolled up to reveal soft tuffs of golden-blond hair on his forearms. His neatly groomed, smooth blond locks caught the sun as I blinked up at him. He looked like a skier standing on a mountaintop then. He was the most beautiful, wholesome looking man I'd ever seen.

"I'm Jack," he said. "Who are you?"

We talked over the bushes. We didn't say much. He wasn't an intellectual, he was more of a creative spirit. He was mellow and calm. He was an actor, just finished a play, and was spending his unemployment relaxing in Brooklyn, renting an apartment from friends. He did a little carpentry to get by. I was welcome to come by and hang out. It would be fun to talk. I seemed really nice. He seemed really nice too. We should get together and be nice together. What a nice idea!

I returned the next day and he invited me into the backyard. It was another sun-drenched Indian summer day and the more we talked, the more I liked him. Up close, I realized he was a lot older than I'd thought. He had little wrinkles around his eyes and his mouth, and when he laughed, he looked old, over 40 for sure. I asked his age and he hesitated, then told me he was 34. Did age matter, he asked? Of course it didn't. We had so much in common.

We talked every day for hours about everything and nothing. He gave me a gift: a doeskin Indian armband, which he said had special significance to him. He couldn't wait to introduce me to his friends. He wanted to take me to meet them. We'd have lunch with them at his favorite Manhattan restaurant and he would teach me about vegetarianism. I couldn't believe my good fortune. It seemed too good to be true, which put me a little on guard but not terribly. He was so darn nice, so caring. Yes, he was a little old, but he was so handsome and so polite. It took him a few days before he even gave me a kiss. Clearly, Amos was a mistake; Jack was the one I'd been waiting for.

True to his word, Jack took me to Manhattan one day to meet his friends. As it turned out, what he meant by having lunch with his friends was bringing me to Brownie's on 7th Avenue, where actors he knew worked tables. When he approached two of them, they seemed irked at first, as if they weren't expecting him. They looked over at me, and one of them walked away. Jack finally dragged another one to our table, but after a hasty greeting, the friend hurried off, never to be seen again. Jack pretended it never happened. He turned his attention back to me. Did I like the brown rice?

I was mystified: he'd either lied to me or didn't realize his friends weren't really his friends.

When I got back to Sheepshead Bay I had a weird sense that I should not have let him drive me into the city in the first place. After my hitchhiking heroics with the religious nut, I should have known better than to get into a vehicle with a man I didn't know that well. Some information was missing in the Jack picture, and I knew it.

The experience at the restaurant bothered me. Were the waiters really his friends? Maybe they were just busy waiting tables? From my perspective, he walked up to a group of people who didn't want to see him and talked one of them into saying hello to his date. I didn't want to believe it, but that's how it looked. It finally dawned on me that there was something creepy about Jack, and it wasn't just that he was dating a 15-year-old.

At moments, it was as if I was the adult and he was the boy who had not yet learned the ways of the world. I couldn't understand how a man his age could be as impractical as he was. He complained I was cynical and over-sophisticated for my age. He acted shocked by my candor about sex and taken aback when I pointed out the flaws in his effusively unrealistic fantasies about running away together. He said that I was smarter than he was and that I understood life more deeply, and encouraged me to talk even more. So I did.

Sexually, he was very passive. He kissed me a few times, little dry, close-mouthed pecks. I was the one making suggestive comments and luring him to depravity. He took great pride in his expensive new waterbed, but all we ever did on it was lie there in our clothes and have long conversations about his acting career.

Only once did we remove our clothes. I took mine off first, and he undressed awkwardly too. I was waiting and waiting for him to do something. I offered to blow him but he seemed embarrassed and uneasy, as if he'd never had a blowjob, so I didn't.

He had a short thick uncircumcised cock which stirred to life only briefly then shrank back, pink and soft. He tried rubbing it against me but that didn't work either. I'd never seen an uncut cock before. It was crumply where it should have been smooth, but the foreskin was strangely cool, like a soft, cozy hood. I would have played with it for hours but he was embarrassed about being soft and got dressed again quickly. We never spoke of it again, nor did we ever again try to make love.

I didn't know what to make of him. He kept talking about us being together permanently and said he loved me. Settling down with a man was the very last thing on my mind, especially one so sexually repressed. The harder he pressed for forever, the more I wanted to get out of there. There was no denying he was handsome but under his good looks, there was something really weird that I could not define.

I couldn't pin him down on anything. He had drifted from place to place, depending on people for favors, mostly unemployed and indifferent about it, doing some acting here, some carpentry there. His prior relationship history was a sacred mystery. He said he was too much of a gentleman to kiss and tell. He talked about having a ton of friends and contacts but no one ever called or sent letters. The landlord wasn't his friend either, just a friendly landlord. Jack didn't seem to know how to make distinctions between facts and fictions and half-truths. The way he told his story, it all made sense, but if I questioned anything, gaping holes appeared everywhere.

When school started, it gave me an easy out. I had to walk in the opposite direction from his place to get there, and when I did see him, complained that I had too much homework to get out much.

But it was inevitable that our paths would cross, since he was just down the street. One evening as I was dragging a shopping cart of groceries home, I saw him playing catch with his landlord's young daughters right where I would pass. He seemed so engrossed with them, I thought I could slip by unnoticed, but he spotted me. In seconds, Jack was at my side.

"This is the girl I told you about," he called out to his landlord.

"Where have you been? I want to cook you dinner!" he said in a low voice to me, so no one could overhear. "Come to my house Friday night, I want to cook something really special for you, ok? I've never cooked for you. I want to cook you something you'll never forget."

He'd never been so pushy before. I didn't know how to say no to his face so I accepted the invitation and hurried home. Spending a Friday night alone with Jack didn't seem like a great idea. I brooded over it all week then decided I was being an idiot, there was nothing wrong with him. It was all in my head.

When I got there on Friday, he'd cleaned the place up and food was cooking on the stove. He'd shut the lights and lit candles. I sat down in obscurity at a small table set with shiny silverware and polished wineglasses. The atmosphere was tense and quiet. Maybe it was because we hadn't talked for a while. He tried to get me to drink some wine, but I suddenly got anxious. What if he drugged the drink? Was he creepy enough to do something like that? I felt ashamed of myself for mistrusting Jack, but all his mish-mashed stories made me nervous around him.

With a flourish, he served his prized appetizer. It was a baked acorn squash fresh from the oven. It was stuffed and topped and drizzled with unknown fillings and spices, layer after layer. It smelled funny to me. I didn't want it. He hovered over me and insisted. He'd made it just for me. Wasn't he going to have any? I wanted to know. Oh yes, but he wanted me to taste mine first.

This instantly reminded me of every poisoning scene in every horror movie I'd ever seen but what could I do? Insult him and reveal that under the cool, witty adolescent exterior I was as hysterical as my mother? I took one bite, then another. The texture was amazing, the presentation was lovely, but a profoundly bitter, acrid medicinal flavor flooded my mouth, nose and throat, instantly sickening me. Migraine pain sliced through my head like an axe. My skull was on fire. My stomach began heaving.

"Are you okay?" Jack asked.

"No," I said, trying not to throw up.

"Eat a little more, it's good for you."

"I have to go." I doubled over from the pain and then ran to the door, half-blind from the migraine. Had he poisoned me? Had he poisoned me??? Was I dying?

By the time I got home, I was sure I'd been poisoned. The bitter taste was still in my mouth. I'd never felt so sick in my life. Every part of me ached. I vomited and vomited again, and then I got diarrhea.

My paranoia said he'd poisoned me. My reason said I'd had stomach aches and food allergies and migraines since early childhood. What if it was psychosomatic? Or what if I had an allergic reaction to a normal spice he'd used, like nutmeg or clove? Or I could have picked up the flu at school. It wasn't possible that Jack would hurt me. I was insane even to think it.

About three days into my misery, my mother came into my room to tell me I had a visitor. Wasn't that nice? It was Jack. He'd come to inquire after my health.

Never before had Jack come to my parents' front door. It was like an unwritten rule of life to play it safe when the relationship was edgy. Not that it was a big secret. My mother knew I was having a relationship with Jack. She didn't know what kind because she didn't like to ask me those questions. She preferred muttering in the background and thwarting me when the whim struck. The way she had registered her disapproval of Jack was to sneak into my closet and throw out the doeskin armband. It sent the message without confrontation.

But on this day she walked him right to my bed, smiling and simpering at his incredible good looks, as I hurriedly smoothed my hair and pulled the blanket up. When she left, Jack sat awkwardly at the edge of my narrow daybed and reached for my hand. I hid it under the blanket.

Undaunted, he asked to hear all about my illness and symptoms. He wanted to know every detail and its emetic particulars. He was deeply solicitous, and so empathetic he seemed to suffer too.

He creeped me the fuck out. I felt sure he had poisoned me. I finally told him I was too sick to talk and asked him to leave.

After that, it was over. We were over. Whatever caused the illness, and even if I was "making a mountain out of a molehill," as my mother often complained, I steered clear of his house. No one else knew about it and I planned to keep it that way. It was just another queasy creepy embarrassing life experience for my box of secrets. I'd never have to see him again.

I thought. I was buying food at a Waldbaum's about a decade later with my lover-of-the-moment, Bill, when I saw a bizarre figure on the canned foods aisle, plodding the aisle like a zombie, bumping into shelves and mumbling to himself. He seemed to be conversing with people in his head, or at least listening to them intently. His hair looked processed, and a cheap dye-job gave it a green tint under the fluorescent lights.

It was Jack. What the fuck had happened to him? He had aged twice as fast as a mortal should. He'd ruined his silky blond hair. His finely etched skin had become a mask of wrinkles, as if he'd had all the moisture in him vacuumed out from the inside.

I pulled Bill aside. "I have to talk to that man."

"Him?" Bill was incredulous.

"Yes, it's something from my childhood."

I stormed over to Jack, filled with an overwhelming urge to confront him. After all this time, suddenly I had to know. Had he poisoned me or was it all my imagination? Was he the evil one or was I, for thinking him dangerous in the first place.

He didn't recognize me. He didn't even see me. He looked right through me.

"Jack?" I said, now a little uncertain. "You're Jack, right?"

"Yes." He nodded. Then he hesitated, as if he wasn't sure who had answered for him.

Bill stood protectively at my side, fists clenched, ready for a fight even though he didn't know what was going on.

It was too late for answers. Jack had vacated the premises. His radar was tuned to another frequency. I'd never know the truth because he probably didn't know it either anymore.

"Let's go," I said to Bill. He didn't ask me to explain. He was good that way. We pushed our cart to a cash register and paid.

That was the last time I saw Jack.

❧ Citizen Perverted Poet ☙

⌘

Ididn't know how emotionally exhausted or hurt I felt by the time I started at the new high school but a couple of weeks into the semester, I began to wake from my fugue of adolescent angst. My sense of shame and anxiety had mushroomed into full-fledged existential crises. I didn't know how I felt about anything, least of all myself. The summer was a disaster, my choices of partners idiotic, my parents unbearable, and I was flat broke in fucking Brooklyn. I was just another nameless, pimple-faceless teen lost inside life's world of pain.

My burst of enthusiasm for boys was gone. I didn't want anyone to touch me. I didn't want boys near me because I didn't trust myself near them. They'd never understand how I felt about sex. No one could. My boundaries were broken so early in life, I practically didn't have any. I could have sex with everyone I met but just because I could didn't mean I should, especially not when real risks and complications were involved. Besides, it was always the boys who had the orgasms, not me. There was only one way to guarantee stress-free joyful orgasms and that was to have sex with myself.

I liked it. I was throbbing with lust all the time. It was my secret life, the life I never told anyone about, the one I lived in my head where, late at night, after the house fell silent, I let my imagination run wild. It was all bondage and more bondage, using scarves and bits of rope to enact my fantasies, and captivity and medical examinations and piss games, the smell of leather or the feel of fur or silk luxuriance against my naked skin, with a convoluted drama in my head worthy of a movie script. Those visions were my precious secrets. I didn't know what they meant, only that they held magical dominion over me, transporting me to a place that was of me and yet so far away from myself that everything there felt fresh and free.

Daily life was surreal, disorienting but not bad, not threatening, more like walking through a funhouse where nothing scares you but the uneven floors and distorting mirrors make you more cautious. I'd stepped through an economic class Looking Glass and into a tidier, safer middle class life. After years of going to schools in poor neighborhoods with a factory approach to learning, tiny budgets and beleaguered teachers, my new high school was rich with opportunities. Teaching supplies abounded, teachers were enthusiastic and warm, and the premises were modern and clean. Walking to school was pleasant now, no longer a minefield of thugs and exhibitionists.

Right off the bat, I was placed in an honors English class with a teacher who loved poetry. Not the stuffy bullshit poetry I'd been forced to read in junior high, with flowery verses by virginal old ladies and wistful reflections on mortality by men in stiff coats. Modern poetry. Raw, belligerent poetry. I'd never heard poetry like that. It sent me on hunts to bookstores, where I found smudgy copies of broadsheets and chapbooks filled with the scrawls of post-modern beatniks and revolutionary Buddhists and unashamed homosexuals like Allen Ginsberg and other people who weren't afraid to tell the truth.

I realized that poetry was sexy. Not sexy like it turned me on. Sexy like it was drenched with sexuality. At least all the best poetry was. I'd tried my hand at poetry in private, labored to write stiff lines like the Victorians. Now I saw that it didn't have to be that way. I didn't have to write about daisies. I could write about cocks and pussies.

I was a poet! That's what was wrong with me. It explained my over-active sexual imagination. Since the age of 12, I'd been writing down thoughts and observations about everyone around me. It was one of my numerous secret hobbies, one I'd hidden from the world better than I hid porn from my parents. My teacher, a buoyant, funny man, got me to share my writing and encouraged me to read my poems in class. That semester, I think he convinced us we were all poets, or could be, if we opened our eyes wider to life.

Until then, I'd always assumed I would grow up to be either an actress or a pianist. I'd studied piano since the age of 8, and my teachers thought I had enough talent to make a career out of it. I dreamt of being an actress, perhaps a star of the musical stage. I practiced for my Broadway debut in front of a mirror in my mother's home every day, from age six to about 10 or 11. I'd throw towels around me as capes and put the record of *The Sound of Music* or *South Pacific* on the portable stereo, and belt out the entire soundtrack, taking all the parts.

Some times, I'd play hit singles on 45s. I loved to screech "STOP! In the Name of Love" dramatically, holding the pose as my imaginary fans roared. My favorite song of all was "Born Too Late," which I believed to be the story of my life. "Born too late for him to notice me, to him, I'm just a kid...." It was my anthem.

Only problem: I hated the spotlight. It gave me the heebie-jeebies when people gave me that look of expectation, like I had the answer to their existential crises. If they only knew how confused I was inside, I thought. If only they knew how fucked up I was. I wasn't made to be among people. I was more of an observer, a voyeur. I preferred watching life from the sidelines, seeing other people do weird or dangerous things but minimizing my own risks. I didn't want to have spotlights on me and people scrutinizing me, and I didn't want to read silly lines from bad scripts, either.

When I fantasized about being an actress, I saw myself waking up one day admired, beloved, respected, with a personal dresser at my side to ensure I was constantly beautiful, while men fell over themselves, vying to worship at the glorious actress' feet. What I never fantasized about were all the things you have to do to make it in the acting business. Like auditioning. Or getting in front of cameras. Or even living up to other people's expectations. Those things petrified me. As for music, it was becoming obvious that I would never be great. I didn't have the talent to become a star. Knowing that the highest I could aim for was being an accompanist or a music teacher sucked the life out of my fantasy of receiving bouquets of roses from handsome men in tuxedos for my tender rendition of a Chopin waltz.

No, I was a poet. It was the first adult occupation that felt possible to me. I would be a poet and write deep verse that would wrench people's hearts, and I would do it in isolation, from the sidelines, at a distance from life. My life would be short and tragic yet filled with sublime love affairs and moments of romantic ecstasy that would be the envy of all when I translated them into moving lines that made old men weep. I'd get dirty with life but not too dirty. I would always be able to slip away into that space where my mind would turn shit to gold and pain to majesty.

I was only 15 but I'd had enough of the messiness of life. My parents were a mess. Men were a mess. Everyone was a mess. I was the biggest mess of all, what with a broken pussy and a chronic inability to get what I wanted. I was fundamentally unlovable. I was born to fail at love. Make that "tragically fail." I would therefore get as much experience as I possibly could, but not get too involved with anyone. I would have romances, but I would never get married. I'd fuck all the men I wanted, but I'd never get pregnant or settle down. I'd live in a million places but never plant roots. I'd just live from one moment to the next the way poets did. I would seek out experience and avoid banal commitments. Commitment was the end of experience. Real poets don't have mortgages.

I was on my own voyage, purified by new poetic purpose. I was above it all – or maybe to the side of it all, although sometimes I felt like I was under it all. All I knew was that the world was not my stage – I was in the wings making notes, the melancholy poet describing the passion of life from the sidelines, fated forever to be alone, a shadowy figure with a sad smile. Yep, that was me.

At least it was for a whole month, and then my pussy was back in the saddle again.

೮ Lust for Leon ೮

⌘

Looking back, and despite the hormonal storm that seized me since first menstruating, what really made me want to push the bounds of sex was a combination of two factors.

First, I was a lonely and emotionally abused child who felt un-loved at home, so I craved affection desperately, no matter its source. If someone was nice to me, I liked them. It didn't go deeper than that.

Second, my mind was swimming with ideas I got from books. My parents weren't role models for me so even as a child, I built a kind of moral system modeled on lessons learned from French and Russian writers, especially Guy de Maupassant, whose tales of kind-hearted whores, bastard children, forbidden affairs and social hypocrisy about sex enchanted me.

So while I responded to affection immediately, I secretly yearned for the types of sophisticated love affairs I had read about. I had no interest in fucking per se, not even that entire year I spent hounding older boys until one finally did the deed with me. What I had wanted was to get fucking over with so I could enjoy an adult romantic life, filled with ecstasy and ago-ny.

My experiences with Amos and Jack were neither. They were more like blisters on my vagus nerve. Vaughn too. I suspected he gave me Chloe as bait, to lure me in to have sex with him.

Now it seemed like he felt I owed him for allowing me to caress her soft nipples and kiss her cupid-bow lips. He'd intimated that he was sure sooner or later he would find the chink in the armor that led to my pussy. His sarcastic jokes and attempts to get a rise out of me put me on edge, so I steered clear of him for a while.

I had noticed there were amazing numbers of good looking boys at the new high school. It astonished me how handsome some of them were. Apparently, while I was joining riots and marching in protests at Erasmus, the boys of Sheepshead Bay had been playing sports and buffing up to look gorgeously hunky for their age. They were cleaner and more pampered, smoother and better dressed than they'd been at Erasmus. But.

I didn't want to get off my own trip. So I hung out with a couple of high school girls just like me: unpopular, pot-smoking, disaffected Jewish girls. We talked morosely about the sex we weren't having and critiqued boys we'd never date while scanning Cosmo for sex tips and make-up ideas.

One day, a girl told us how she caught her father brushing his teeth late one night, after there had been a lot of noise in her parents' bathroom. She was sure they'd been having oral sex.

Confessions like this always made me wonder about people. Her parents were the last people in the world I could imagine having oral sex, both of them middle-aged and out of shape and very bland, ordinary and plain people. She claimed that when she questioned her dad about it, he merely grinned at her and slipped back in the bedroom. The thought that a child could even raise the subject of sex, much less oral sex, was so cool to me it pushed me a tiny emotional step forward. Fat old people still had sex. It was amazing.

With winter coming on, I was also spending more time with my own parents. We never talked about sex, or anything that was particularly interesting. On the other hand, they never talked when the television was on, so I could spend an entire evening engrossed in torrid romances in my head while donating my body to family time.

When Robin, the girl who sat next to me in poetry class invited me to hang out with her clique shortly before Christmas, I was dubious. She was fresh-faced and wholesome, dressed in colorful, cheery outfits and had flawless teeth and skin. She was far too straight to be interesting, I thought, but she was supersmart and we had a lot of fun joking together in class, so I agreed to show up.

Her friends met at yet another basement apartment inhabited by yet another adolescent male. When I knocked on the door, a low-key boy named Manny politely shook my hand in the vestibule before leading me into a dark cavern with day-glo posters on the walls. A seating area was arranged as a stoner mosh-pit with a hookah set out on the coffee table.

Robin was on the couch amidst a sea of handsome boys who were cheering her on as she sucked down a joint in a lung-busting super-toke that made everyone, myself included, shout YAY. Obviously, Robin was not too wholesome. She was just right!

Someone passed me a pipe and then a joint and before long, I was on the couch with Robin, and we were laughing and getting high. They were incredibly mellow, and they were all my age. This was new and strangely comfortable. I could let down my guard with them. They all seemed really nice.

Robin dragged me to a corner. She was filled with wonderful surprises. Her sense of humor killed me, she had strong opinions about life, she was a staunch feminist, and she was uninhibited about sex. Under that supremely wholesome presentation, the product inside was deliciously wicked and delightfully wise.

After a few hours, things quieted down and Robin went to sit with her boyfriend. I realized there was one boy who'd been there all night that I hadn't met. He was off by himself, strumming a guitar, having a more meditative high than the rest of us. He seemed different from us too, older, more serious.

"Who's that?" I quietly asked Manny.

"That's my friend Leon," Manny said. "He's a year older than us, but I've known him all my life. He lives down the street. You should meet him. Come on."

Manny introduced us, and I sat down to hear him play the guitar. His riffs were soulful and sweet. He was self-taught. Music was his life. The more he talked, the more handsome he grew. He was the real thing. He was sexy and he was a real musician. Fair blonde hair stuck out of the top of his pale blue shirt. He was tall, a little thick and very masculine. He looked more like 18 than 16. He had a red beard and hurt, gentle eyes. He didn't smile much. His air of sadness touched my heart.

We talked for a while, as he strummed some chords and then he asked, "Would you give me a back massage?"

"Yessss." I suddenly knew I wanted to touch him, to feel his shoulders and thighs, to kiss his lips. It was more than wanting. I needed to feel his body against mine.

I followed him to the couch and he lay down, telling me it was okay to sit on him, and please would I rub his shoulders. I straddled his spine and dug in, wordlessly. I felt the shape of his muscles through his shirt. His back was solid and strong. I pushed my thumbs into the knots as deep as I could. He writhed a little and I clamped my thighs around his firm young ass, the seam of my jeans digging into my pussy. Every time I rubbed him, my jeans rubbed me.

He smelled so good I wanted to dive into him and be covered with his smell. Everything about him was so beautiful, so perfect, so sexy, so masculine. He was hairy in all the right places, and his beard was so soft it was like velvety fur. His long blonde hair fell in shimmering strands. His ass was full and round like a girl's, but his legs were pure man. For all that I was feeling, it was like having sex in plain sight. Nobody watching knew I was on the edge of orgasm the whole time.

Within a few days, I was his girlfriend. I was incredibly happy about it. He was nothing like any of the boys I'd known. He was so serious about his music, it was all he ever thought about. I did not entirely mind that he placed our relationship second to his relationship with his guitar. That made sense to me, and made me respect him, and even envy him. His passion was so intense. I wished my passion for writing was as strong.

It wasn't perfect. He was not a reader, so outside of music and mutual friends, we had little to talk about. He spent most of his time in his room practicing, and both of us were broke, so there were no dream dates or exciting adventures. Still, I couldn't complain about Leon, even if secretly I was a little bored, because the things we did have in common made up for everything else.

We were both stoners and since Leon was generous with his smoke, I was very grateful for the ready source of highs. Best of all, though, was the sex. Leon was perfect for me at that moment in my life quite simply because he did not push me. Until then, sex was a bewilderment of clumsy advances and awkward caresses, confusing needs and weird sensations. But Leon let me do what I wanted. This took my pussy off the table, both as a conversation piece and a commoditized object, and let me hide the shameful truth that I wasn't as fuckable as I looked. Instead, his ever-ready virility meant that any time I was in the mood, he was in the mood. And, if I wasn't in the mood, he could always strum his guitar. It gave me a sense of control I'd never felt before.

I spent hours touching his naked body. Caressing him, exploring him, watching his dick get hard, then shoot, then grow soft, then get hard again after a while so the cycle could repeat. I'd watch his balls crawl under the light scattering of red fur between his legs, and I'd watch the muscles on his torso stretch as he arched and succumbed to orgasm.

For the first time, lust filled my loins with a near-painful intensity. Pangs of desire throbbed in my vagina, almost excruciatingly painful and yet wondrously deep throbs that seemed to explode from my core. It was the desire I'd dreamt of but I had no idea it felt like that, so physical, so urgent, so all-consuming, so compulsive. Just thinking about the way his cock got hard made me need to jerk off. Again and again and again and again, with this new lustiness throwing me into a state of such dreamy joy that I really didn't ever want to come down and not be horny.

I was still too spooked to try fucking again. I was happy to throw myself into a fugue of lust with Leon and then race home to jerk off as if there wouldn't be time to cum when I grew up. The more he bored me, the less I talked to him, the more I focused on worshiping his nakedness with my hands and seeing how he reacted to the sensations I gave him, and then jerking off to the memories of what we'd done.

After a few months, he made some mild complaints. He wanted more – more blowjobs, and fucking too but, by then, things had changed for me emotionally. Sexually, I still desired him. The masturbation marathons were still in full bloom. But as a boyfriend, not so much. He was a little dull. I'd sworn I'd go to any limits for the sake of love, but I wasn't in love with Leon. I'd never been in love with him. I'd fallen in love with his sexiness. It wasn't the same. I stuck to what worked for me.

One day, about six months into our relationship, Leon called me on the phone. He announced we were over: he had to break up with me. I was shocked. He explained that a girl we both knew, Ophelia, had tried to commit suicide the night before. My heart froze.

Ophelia had been wooing me as a friend for months. We met in a dance class. She said she was a professional ballerina. I knew she was too chubby to be a ballerina but I didn't question her. She had light scars on her wrists from a multitude of self-inflicted cuts and when she looked at you, you weren't sure if she saw you or not. She was the kind of person who didn't think she'd successfully entered a room unless everyone in it turned to look at her. The burgeoning friendship came to an abrupt end when I caught her in several lies. I wouldn't talk to her after that. So she called Leon.

He told me she called him late last night. She had locked herself in a closet. Only he could save her. Valiantly he raced there on bicycle to rescue her from the closet. She flew into his arms. He spent the night. Something told me he fucked her too.

"But you know…" I stumbled, "she's always threatening to commit suicide and never does? I mean, you know she's really, really," I searched for the word, "THEATRICAL."

Leon said, "She's sensitive."

"Why did she call my boyfriend in the first place?"

"Urm…." He got suspiciously quiet.

"Isn't it strange that, out of the blue, she would call my boyfriend?"

"Well, urm," he hemmed and hawed. "We've been talking for a few weeks."

"You mean you've been dating her behind my back?" I felt all cold inside.

"It's not like that," he said.

"What's it like?"

"She needs me, Gloria," he said. "She's weak. She needs me."

I couldn't argue with that. I was not weak. If he needed a weak girl, we never should have been together in the first place. I heard the clear implication: she needed him and I didn't. Wasn't it what I'd always said about myself anyway? I didn't need him because I didn't need people, not the way other people needed people.

I told myself all the stuff we tell ourselves when someone dumps us. It wouldn't have lasted anyway. I didn't want a boy who didn't want me. He lied to me.

It still hurt. But not too bad.

❧ Crushing Feldman ☙

⌘

Hippie philosophy spread its legs wide open at the beginning of the 1970s. Times were still a-changing politically (or so we thought). The Sexual Revolution was still on (or so we thought). It was easy to get contraceptives and doctors could cure all the known STDs – which we naively assumed meant the permanent end of sexually transmitted diseases. It was far out. It was groovy. It was the era of free love and sex was safer than it had ever been.

Among hip people, sexuality was all new. You could sleep with someone you met five minutes ago and it wasn't any less legitimate than wooing them and waiting months. In fact, waiting seemed absurd. Forcing yourself to behave unnaturally was all a product of straight culture, an artificial construct that self-respecting free-lovers rejected as brainwashing and propaganda. You didn't have to love someone until you died to have a good time with them in life. You didn't have to marry them. You didn't have to love, honor and cherish them for any longer than the time you were together. You could follow your heart wherever it led, to any bed where you were welcome. If more than one person was in that bed even better. Spread the love, baby. There were no rules, except to enjoy the trip that life brought to you.

The unforeseen break-up with Leon didn't so much sadden me as give me a new perspective on relationships. I wasn't angry or jealous about Leon fucking Ophelia. Sex was just sex. It didn't re-align the earth's polarity. It was his lie that upset me. He didn't have to stop our sex life because he needed to take care of a broken birdie, did he? Had he told me, we could have worked it out and I could have been sleeping with other boys. I'd wasted valuable sexy time being monogamous with him and endured hours of listening politely to him practicing guitar when I could have been exploring other penis options. Being faithful to him was some tedious shit.

So I went back to what I was good at: picking random boys who seemed interesting and seeing where it led. First up was an incredibly good looking boy and his not at all good looking best friend. I'd seen them hither and yon around the school, always together. I wanted that good looking boy and I wanted him any way I could have him. But I couldn't get past not-good-looking.

Once not-good-looking noticed me ogling his buddy, he wouldn't leave me alone, coming over to me in the yard every day to ask pointed questions about my sexual experience, pretending he was gathering information for a survey. It was stupid but funny, and I laughed when he took notes about my experience with blowjobs. Good-looking always lingered just out of voice-range, pretending he wasn't watching, and looking better and better to me at this frustrating distance.

Finally, not-good-looking talked me into coming over to good-looking's parents' apartment and showing them both what a blowjob was like. It didn't take a lot of convincing. Giving them blowjobs seemed like another way to make friends, sort of sophisticated and cool, really, to be the kind of hippie who can have sex on first meeting and handle her shit afterwards. I knew that once we got to talking, I'd find a way to snag a date with good-looking. I was always good at talking my way into and out of things, and good-looking now seemed a kind of guy I could talk into bed. Obviously, these boys were as experimental and fun-loving as me.

Off we went, but before I got too far past the entry foyer in good-looking's house, they stopped and turned around. Behind them, I saw an all-white living room with plastic slipcovers over everything, a living room so pristine and antiseptic it unnerved me for a second. Signaling each other, they lowered their pants, side by side. I dropped to my knees and gave them little sample blowjobs, thinking this was definitely one of the more radical experiences I'd had, and how it was extremely cool to have two penises to play with, when without further discussion, they both hoisted their pants back up and led me back to the door.

"It's over?" I asked.

"Yes, yes. Goodbye, Gloria." Click.

I walked home in outraged grief. What the hell just happened?

It was worse when they avoided me at school. They vanished from all the places where I used to see them, and once when I spotted good-looking down a hall, he walked away so fast, it was plain he didn't want to talk to me.

A part of me was anguished. They were right to treat me like that. I was a cheap tramp, easy for any man to use. Another part of me despised them for being so straight. I was living up to my ideals and they used me. Unenlightened bastards. Sexist motherfuckers! On the other hand, maybe I was just a whore, an easy target for anyone. Either way, my life was a hollow sham.

I stopped dating for a little while but it only drove my imagination wild. My mild fascination with male teachers at high school now blossomed into obsessive sexual fantasies. They could understand me! They were mature, sophisticated men. They would play sex games with me without judgment. I saw it all in my head.

My kinkiest fantasies revolved around a warm, witty history teacher in his late 20s named Harry Feldman whose pants hung low and tight around his ass and were so spacious in front you couldn't help but wonder if there was an elephant in that room.

Mr. Feldman had a special fondness for me and Robin, and we regularly stayed late after class to talk to him. We had a special fondness for making lame schoolgirl jokes about him behind his back and obsessively gossiping about the many mysteries that were Mr. Feldman. Did Feldman have a girlfriend? If so, what did she look like? Did he fuck her? What kind of woman would Feldman fuck? What kind of woman would fuck HIM? OMG! Can you imagine Feldman fucking? Scrub inner eyes, scrub inner eyes! (Though in secret, I wanted to imagine Feldman fucking...fucking me, that is.)

I remember Feldman most vividly, though, from two episodes in my senior year, the first from winter 1972. I'd been carrying an erotic torch for him since eleventh grade, when I had worshiped him from the front row. He still popped up in private masturbatory fantasies. But in reality, I was only one of Feldman's many fangirls. We were the ones who lingered after the bell to make moon eyes, confiding our personal problems to him, claiming homework problems, or requesting clarifications of the finer points of our lessons (my own specialty). Fangirls had an uneasy alliance. On one hand, we were the only ones who understood why we were his fans in the first place; on the other, we were competitors for Feldman's attention.

I was on my way to school when I spotted a fellow crusher who paused to say hi and sniff out some gossip I might not have yet heard. She was a pale girl with a sunken chest and owlish eyes. Our chat rapidly devolved into a Feldman love-fest as we talked about how wonderful he was, how handsome, how smart.

"I love him," I said, by which I meant I'd give anything to have sex with him.

"I am *in love* with him," she said, pursing her lips.

I stiffened. Was she saying that my love was inferior to her love? Her eyes shimmered strangely. "I want to have his baby," she said.

I gasped. If this was a contest she just won. She loved him way more than I did. Have his baby? She was barely 16. Had her unrequited love for Feldman driven her to madness? I'd read *Anna Karenina*. I knew what happened to women who let their lust run away with them. According to my reading, all uncontrolled passions ended in death or disfigurement – Romeo and Juliet, Antony and Cleopatra, Abelard and Heloise. They were like lessons on how to avoid letting your passions get the best of you.

That conversation squashed my lust for Feldman. I don't know if it died because I realized that another girl loved him more that I ever could or because I was afraid I'd turn into her if I spent too much time obsessing over him. Either way, her fantasies about him ruined mine. Now I had to think of him as a potential baby-maker, driving women to madness, rather than a witty teacher with a big dick.

On the last day of school, in June of 1972, Mr. Feldman invited me to stop by his classroom after the bell to sign my yearbook and say goodbye in private. This was a treat. He'd offered the same sweetness to Robin and was still scribbling in her book when I walked in.

Many things had happened since I first crushed on Feldman. In addition to the fangirl's frightening confession, another teacher, Max Lerner, had been whispering unflattering details of Feldman's private life in my ear. And then there had been the summer of 1971 that had blasted through my life, embedding its debris deep in my psyche.

Still, old lusts die hard and it was sad knowing I'd never ever get a chance to live out any bondage fantasies with him or see him in the loin cloth he'd worn in one particularly enjoyable fantasy scenario.

After Robin left, Feldman fussed over my book for a while, then stood up from his desk and leaned back casually against the blackboard, as I'd seen him do so many times during class. He beckoned to me to join him, so I did. He put his arm out. I thought he wanted a goodbye hug. I put my arms up and in seconds he enfolded me completely. He wrapped his arms so tightly around me, I felt swallowed up in him. Then he bent his head down and gave me the longest, deepest, most passionate kiss I'd ever gotten, thrusting his tongue so deep in my throat I almost gagged.

"I always wanted to do that," he said once he released me.

"You did?" I was stunned.

"God yes. Are you ok?"

"Yes," I said, "yes, ok. Yes."

"I'll miss you," he said. It looked like he was going to say something more.

"Me too," I said. "I gotta go now."

It was so unexpected and so spontaneous. It was, in fact, sweet. It was no secret I crushed on him, and he fulfilled my fantasy in the best way possible. Mr. Feldman tongue-kissed me! What a crazy great way to say goodbye. I couldn't wait to tell Robin. It would make a great story, and we would giggle over it for weeks. But deep inside, it felt like a waste of a great tongue kiss. My emotions had dried up. He didn't even know who he was kissing. I wasn't the girl he knew in eleventh grade anymore. He hadn't kissed the real me. I didn't know if I would ever let anyone kiss the real me again.

❧ Teacher Lerner ☙

⌘

Buried in one of the school corridors was an armored door to a supply room operated by a part-time teacher and full-time roué named Max Lerner. I passed it several times a day to attend classes, sometimes detouring from other routes just to cruise him as he supervised student traffic.

Max was darkly handsome, almost movie star good looking, with thick brown hair he wore swept up off his forehead in a romantic tangle, fierce brown eyes, an aquiline nose and thin cold lips. He reminded me of the actor James Mason a little, and the way we spoke re-enforced the impression. His elocution was so meticulous he sounded more like a Shakespearean actor than a boy from Brooklyn. He was 26, finishing up a graduate degree in the sciences and writing the great American novel. He took the lab job to pay rent and tuition as he labored to become Hemingway. To prepare for his future fame, he dressed like a writer, in poet shirts and tight bellbottoms that hugged his crotch as tightly as he wished everyone would. Oh Max. I found him irresistible.

He wasn't exactly a bad person. He had mad quality – great taste in everything, from music to art, to clothes and foods; he was absurdly well-educated both in sciences and literature; he had a devilish sense of humor, both dry and very wicked. He was an edge-player in bed, not with any toys or devices or complex scenarios – he played the psychological edges, making things seem risky all the time. Tutoring an eager 15-year-old student became his favorite game.

That a man like him was interested in me was both a revelation and satisfying evidence that I wasn't a whore, but – as Max saw me – a free-spirited sexual adventurer, defying the norms of outdated convention and foolish traditions. He was the most worldly man I'd ever dated. He had a lavishly furnished bachelor pad in Flatbush, filled with books and souvenirs from extensive travels abroad. The art in the kitchen was pure Max. Literally. Overhanging the table nook was a copper *repoussé* tribute to his penis, carved in exquisite detail, down to the veins on his massive prick. It was an homage, he admitted, from a former girlfriend.

Max treated me like the sexiest girl in the world. It seemed sort of funny to me, not real, more his fantasy of me than me, but I liked it. I'd drop in on him when I had breaks and he would steal me away to some bookcases in the back of the lab to gently kiss me, trembling with desire as he whispered about the trouble we'd be in if someone came through the door. Then he'd kiss me harder.

The drama was fun. I'd creep into his office at odd times, tiptoeing to where he sat and silently rub the back of his neck in greeting. He'd pretend he hadn't heard the door open and close, but he was usually hard by the time I reached him, and groaned softly when I touched him.

He talked to me. About everything. He gossiped about the other teachers and, upon learning that I had a crush on his pal Feldman, set about tarnishing his friend in my mind. Max was a free spirit but it peeved him that I was attracted to another teacher.

Max introduced me to the concept of clandestine relationships. They fascinated me. They were, as I saw them, illicit, underground and thus almost unbearably romantic relationships.

They were wrong. Otherwise you would not have to hide your love. Oh, how romantic to have to hide your love, I thought! How right it was to be wrong for the sake of love! How adult!

The reason Max and I had to hide was less romantic: he'd lose his job if school administrators knew he was dating a student. I thought it was a terribly unfair rule at the time, and he agreed with me, but he'd signed a contract. The legal aspect of this pissed me off. Why did school administrators, pressured by parents, get to decide whether I could sleep with a teacher? As far as I was concerned, the fact that irrational prudes tried to control me was all the justification I needed to refuse to be controlled.

Max's biggest contribution to my sexual development was that he taught me how to give a proper blowjob. Until then, and despite dispensing advice to other girls, my concept of fellatio was that you kissed the head and licked it a little, maybe sucked it once or twice and you were done. Max corrected my misconceptions.

"Take it all the way in, as far it will go, yes, yes, like that," he'd say, sprawled on the bed. "Lick it all over... Hold it and lick it...then...yes...stroking is good...yes... Suck on it, suck harder, yes, like that, suck like thaaaaaa," he'd murmur, drifting into bliss.

I enjoyed getting Max's sex lessons as much as he enjoyed giving them. I wanted to be a good lover, I wanted to know how to drive men crazy with lust and how to make them happy in bed. Our bedroom game, of him as the teacher and me his avid student, was easy and deliciously kinky to me. I couldn't wait to get into bed with him.

He never pressured me for intercourse, and was content with oral sex, worshiping my breasts, and being sensually dominant with me. His cock lived up to its engraving: it was big, thick and lovely, a dark cherry red, almost purple when fully engorged.

And his body was hairy, oh my god, was he hairy. I don't know if I always had a fetish for hairy men but, if not, under Max's spell my fetish detonated. Thick black fuzz spread from his thick toes to his sharp chin. It coiled fiercely around his genitals and nipples. I could have kissed every curlicue and sucked it into my mouth. I swooned when his hairy sweaty flesh rubbed against mine.

After we had sex, he'd talk to me about books, music, other world cultures. He was a voracious and critical consumer of art culture. He gave me books to read, and recommended authors. At the Brooklyn College bookstore, he encouraged me to fill my basket, and then paid for two full shopping bags of books for me. No gift ever made me so happy.

Our encounters were intense and sporadic – rushing to be together, throwing ourselves into each other's arms, and then not seeing each other again for weeks at a time. Some of it was because it was hard for us to coordinate schedules, especially since I had to invent excuses and lies about where I was vanishing to for half a day or an evening. Mostly, though, it was because he was uptight about being seen with me, and worried that people would be hostile to our intergenerational relationship.

It left lots of time for other relationships. I stuck to my pledge to fly solo, opting simply to go with whomever I felt like going with when I wanted some male company. No boyfriend, no monogamy, no expectations, no structure. It felt more natural to me.

❧ Pimple-Popping Porn ❧
and Other Pastimes

⌘

One of my first, most basic understandings about erotic pleasure is that you didn't need a partner to have an orgasm. The sex I had with boys was fun, but the sex I had with myself was funner. Ever since I discovered my happy button at age five, I had turned to masturbation for comfort, release, and mainly for an escape from reality. My fantasies were infinitely more exciting than real life sex, which was all sensation-based. When I masturbated, though, I traveled and transformed and transcended all the boundaries of time (I could be any age), space (I could be anywhere in the world), and endurance (bondage and torture could last for weeks).

I'd wait to hear the sounds of light snores from my parents' bedroom, then rummage through my dresser and closet for ideas. I had a scarf that could serve several purposes – twisted and knotted up for bondage, or draped for sensuality, or tied in strange ways to expose parts of my body. Sometimes I wore my winter boots, because I liked the way the leather felt on my skin. Before I even touched myself, I'd start stoking myself with fantasies, scripting sexy conversations in my head, imagining bizarre fetish scenarios and losing myself completely until I couldn't stand it anymore and wildly jerked off until I came. I could stretch out the fantasies and make them last for weeks, returning nightly to my faceless partners like familiar lovers.

My imagination didn't fail me, but I longed for more. More, more, MORE! Boys had all kinds of porn. They jacked off with anything and everything that they could stick their dicks into. I'd tried massaging and grinding again a wide range of common objects, from shampoo bottles to pillows, but they weren't enough. Plus, I never saw any porn that turned me on. I'd never read an actual book of smut. The closest I'd come was when the boy who wrestled with me at my parents' friends' home repeated a passage from *Fanny Hill* that he'd secretly memorized. The phrase "he manipulated her nipple" instantly burned itself into my memory. I'd conjure it sometimes when I was jerking off. If all porn read like that, maybe a whole book of it would take me over the top.

"Did you know they sell smutty books at the train station?" Robin asked, plumes of pot smoke elegantly steaming from her nostrils one afternoon in my bedroom as I recounted the frustrations of being female.

I knew what she meant: right next to the subway entrance was the ubiquitous candy store/newsstand that flanked MTA stations all along our line. I'd been inside many times, but had never plumbed the racks of magazines.

She passed me the pipe and I sucked down the rest of the bowl.

"They hide them behind the *Playboys*," Robin said with authority. Her dad owned a magazine kiosk. She knew exactly where all the good stuff was hidden.

"OMG. We have to get one."

We pooled our pocket change and headed out, stoned on our asses and laughing uncontrollably. "Porn!" we'd squeal, bending in half from the pain of our delight.

When we got to the Sheepshead Bay Road train station, our body language changed and we began ducking and hiding our faces, like criminals. We were very serious when Robin grabbed a handful of cheap-looking books from behind the glossy sex magazines. We could only afford one, so we started thumbing through them, and then realized there was a problem. Someone was going to have to pay for this shit. Neither of us wanted the job. As we whispered fiercely back and forth, we started laughing again, so much we couldn't stop.

Finally, I grabbed *Blistering Summer* and darted to the counter, where a surly man nodded when I threw down all the money we had, and we ran out of the shop, holding each other up so we wouldn't pass out from laughter. We felt like we'd gotten away with something nasty, procuring our very own book of pornography! It had been so ridiculously easy but we were breathless at our own audacity. *Blistering Summer*! It sounded so hot. We half-raced the half-mile back to my house to open this great work of erotic literature.

The book, predictably, was awful, but it was awful in memorable ways. The big lovemaking scene, for example, was hilariously marred by a detailed description of the acne on the hero's back, and how his pimples oozed and exploding during a rough lovemaking session.

"Ewwwwwwwwwwwwwwww," we shrieked. "BARF!"

We didn't stop reading it. We couldn't. It was so strangely disgusting, we could not help ourselves. Plus there was real fucking in it, unfortunately described perhaps, but real details of people doing it. OH.

The other peculiarity of the book was that one of the female characters had so feverish a fit of horniness that one surrealistic episode ended with her fucking a tree stump. This too sent me and Robin into helpless paroxysms of giggles, but I didn't forget it either because it was the first time it occurred to me that maybe there were other people out there who were as sexually weird, and even weirder, than me. I had never fantasized about trees – but I had fantasized about all kinds of stuff I knew other people would think was twisted and sick. I kind of admired the tree-fucking girl for being so brazen.

After realizing that, amusing though it was, porn was not the solution, Robin shared more from her well of sexual knowledge. Muscle massagers served double duty as female jerk off aids. I should try one. They were easy to get and pretty cheap. A discount variety store on Nostrand Avenue, where I'd previously only shopped for gum and batteries, sold them for a couple of dollars.

I dug out a few dollar bills from my secret stash, and off we went. This time, we were women on a sober mission. She walked ahead to the small appliance aisle and discreetly pointed to the shelf. It amazed me that these tools for females were stacked beside toasters and crock pots, like another small appliance essential for housewives. Robin discretely vanished as I examined the box, mystified by the warning not to use the massager on "unexplained calf pain." I didn't plan to use it on my legs, still the warning made the vibrator sound like a dangerous, even fatal, tool if applied incorrectly.

That night, I couldn't wait for my parents to fall asleep. I didn't know exactly how to use my new toy, but as soon as I pressed its buzzing body between my legs, tingles of pleasure began rushing through me, sensations first so sweet and then so rapturous, it felt like I'd had a revelation. It was more than I'd ever felt between my legs, more than I dreamt I could feel. I was so proud of my intense orgasm, I congratulated myself.

It was a tiny but meaningful change. I felt orgasmically enlightened, uninhibited, and truly sexually self-sufficient. I could control my own ecstasy. Now I felt motivated more than ever to seek out love and adventure. Surely, the peak experience would be to know that level of ecstasy in a man's arms.

The world is a deceptively friendly place to a cute teenage girl. Everywhere I went, there were smiling boys and men, and everywhere there were smiling boys and men, at least one of them would come on to me. I didn't even have to leave the neighborhood to find random swains. Sheepshead Bay overflowed with gregarious males. Chatting could lead to a kiss or more, depending on the chemistry.

There was a memorable afternoon of making out with Seth, a boy who didn't know how to kiss, but did it with such annihilating ferocity it turned me on. I'd seen him around the high school. He was a handsome, sensitive looking boy one grade up from me, with a thick crop of tangled curls. I don't remember how we ended up back in his bedroom, just that he ground me so hard into the bed from head and toe that we left a crater in his bed and my chin and lips hurt for a week.

One afternoon, a long-haired phone company guy in uniform showed up to install a new phone. My mother was off at work, so I welcomed him in. We chatted as he worked, then shared a joint. He offered to come back in a few days with a bag of dope and a free extra phone he would install in my bedroom if I cooked him lunch. I made him an omelet and we ended up making out. I felt like I got a great deal, especially when he then converted the leftover phone parts into a pot pipe for me. I was the only person I ever knew who had a black and blue princess phone pot pipe.

On one desultory shopping trip through Greenwich Village, I met an intelligent older boy who said he was a runaway. He spent most of his days camping by the Cooper Union landmark "Alamo," and we made out there one afternoon, in the shadow of the cube, while he periodically took breaks from kissing to panhandle change from passersby.

Another time, I ended up spending two long afternoons with a boy from Colorado, who told me his entire life story as we sat on his bed, intermittently kissing and groping. He wasn't sure if he was gay or not. After making out for a while, neither of us knew what should come next. I didn't mind if he was bisexual, but he seemed to have a lot more to figure out before we went to bed.

On and on it went, with random acts of eroticism abounding all spring. I don't remember them in meaningful order, much less all the names or brief encounters, just that I danced through a lot of spontaneous kissing and genital-fondling, occasional blowjobs, finger-fucking and a good bit of humping. There was even a make-out session with a girl. Nothing lasted but nothing was unpleasant either, it was just easy, low-key canoodling that seldom went too far. I wasn't finding ecstasy but I was gathering piles of fascinating information about sex. I discovered, among other things, that some of the best looking boys were the worst in bed, while some of the homely ones were studmuffins who knew exactly how to get you off. I didn't like short boys and wasn't strongly attracted to fat boys but it was a short fat boy I paired off with one day who'd given me the best orgasm. That opened my horizons.

Meanwhile, I was flirting with some of the guys in Robin's circle, renewed my on-again, off-again blowjob relationship with Ken, and drifted back to Vaughn's where a bearded newcomer had entered the fold and Chloe was, alas, on her way out.

Between my boundless thirst for erotic adventure, and my tutelage by Max, I felt as friendly towards men as they felt towards me, and on my way to becoming the romantic heroine of my fantasies.

A Sex Education ଔ
in the Catskills

⌘

No eye his future can foretell
No law his past explain
Whom neither Passion may compel
Nor Reason can restrain.
-- "A Rake's Progress"

The road to chaos is paved with impulsive decisions.

I was born into chaos, I lived in chaos, chaos was in my DNA. Nothing really made sense at home. It was my mother's world and it was run by fears. Impulsive decisions were the norm, sometimes in moments of grandiosity, sometimes in moments of anger or aggression. Any failure could be forgiven as weakness and every flaw was only human. Unless it was committed by the youngest daughter, in which case I was demonized. There was a narrative to the household, and my role in it was to be bad.

So I got badder with every passing year. No effort required. I just said what was on my mind. My mother was personally insulted by my view of life. She wanted me in skirts and stockings with make-up and styled hair; I wore army boots, jeans, and work shirts and my hair was a frizzy mane. She wanted me to stay a virgin until married; I defended free love and said virginity was absurd. She wanted unquestioning obedience; she got dirty looks. She wanted me to trust her; not even remotely possible. The only thing my mother and I agreed on was that women could run their own lives. Unfortunately for her, that empowered me to run mine like a steamroller over hers.

Even when I knew better, I'd give in to my whim instead of listening to the nerd in my head. I stayed home as little of the time as possible, sometimes ending up scared half to death by friends whose idea of fun was climbing cliffs in the dark or meeting their dealers in bad neighborhoods in the middle of the night. When boys invited me out, I always went. I never turned anyone down. I was grateful for any excuse to get away. Sometimes, boys pushed me into having sex when I was ambivalent. At least sex was interesting, I thought. Even when it was boring, it was ok. It didn't scare me, and neither did men. It was still better than being at home.

I'd been reading books by and about notorious women, particularly Colette. I wanted to be Colette, a literary woman who had a scandalous reputation for dancing half naked on stage in her youth and indulging in dozens of mad affairs. I wanted to be Simone de Beauvoir, a serious intellectual who never married her glamorously brilliant boyfriend, and lived as a free woman. And I wanted to be Edith Piaf, fucking in the alleys and doorways of Paris, and throwing her heart into ill-fated love affairs with heroic but doomed men. To me, they were geniuses of life, women who really knew how to live. I grieved that I didn't know how to get from where I was – a homely, big-titted, frizzy-haired self-hating nerdy Jewess from Brooklyn – to the glittering world stage.

It helped that I was a good liar, so good, I would help friends out when they needed convincing excuses to get out of trouble or skip a class. My mother was a pathological liar. She firmly believed that most people didn't deserve to know the truth.

Truth, in her experience, was more perilous than a lie, sometimes unwelcome, even downright anti-social. When you lied, you were actually giving people the truth they were prepared to hear or, conversely, the truth you needed them to hear so you could get what you wanted.

We lied to my sister because "she was too sensitive" and we lied to my father because "he would get too upset." Naturally, I lied to everyone, including boys. I didn't want them to know how weird I was, or how much sex I had, or really anything significant about me. I wanted to come and go like a fairy, leaving nothing but a trail of sparkles behind, I guess. And while I told myself I knew the difference between my lies and the truth, looking back now, I don't think I did.

I was also compartmentalized. Since childhood, I organized people in my head into boxes: the good people, the bad people, the interesting people, and the dull ones. Different boxes got different treatment, and different levels of investment. So a nice boy I wasn't terribly attracted to might enjoy a brief erotic contact with me but I wouldn't let it last. Or I'd go out with a boy, but he was more attracted to me than I was to him, and I didn't want to lead him on. Or he was super cute but dumb as a rock. I couldn't see him more than once.

I liked to cut things off quickly and quietly, without any drama. I just moved on and became unavailable. No matter if only the night before, during sexual arousal, I'd told him I loved him. For me, anything said in a moment of passion was meaningless after the passion was over. I didn't even understand why men consistently thought "I love you" meant more than "that was a great time." It was completely irrational to think anyone could genuinely be in love with someone they just met.

I knew there were boys you fell in love with, because I had truly loved Martin. Boys like that hardly ever came along, even though they were the ones you were always longing to meet. When you found one, sex wasn't that important, because there were so many other things connecting you to them – the things you thought and felt, the things you dreamt about, the way you saw the world. A boy you really loved could break your heart with a word or a gesture; his sadness made you sad; he had this power over you that kept you fascinated by his every word and concerned for his every care. My heart stayed true to Martin for many years like that.

Then there were boys like Leon, so sexy you had to be with them or you felt like you'd die, but who, on the other hand, were actually a bit dull outside of bed. They were special too, because the sex was great with them, but it didn't break your heart when they left.

And then there was everybody else. It was nice to be with them, it was fun to have crazy spontaneous adventures with them, but none of them were ever going to be more than an adventure, an episode, a story I could tell when I grew up.

Sometime in late spring, I got a notion to get away for the summer. I needed to make some money. The allowance my mother doled out was barely enough to cover snacks or smokes, so I was always scrounging for jobs. I'd babysat, worked a few part-time clerical jobs off the books, and tutored, but no one would hire me for a real job until I was 16. Except, possibly, for a Catskills hotel which, I'd recently learned from a high school friend, was looking for counselors for their day camp. You had to be 16 to get the job, but they didn't require proof, so if I was willing to lie on the form, and brought my mother with me to back me up, they might hire me.

Well, fuck yeah. I became obsessed with the idea. A job in the Catskills would be perfect: earn money by day, party at night and get away from home. Being a counselor instead of a camper was going to be great. Plus, this was a day camp, so you returned the kids to the parents every evening. Piece of cake! I saw myself leading a bunk of nice kids, teaching arts and crafts, proudly sharing my newly acquired skills at needlepoint and making copper jewelry. They would look up to me and then I'd get to party every night, smoke dope, sing folk songs, and hang out with the other counselors. Best of all, at the end of the summer I'd have a fortune. I was told that parents tipped generously at summer's end, and some counselors went home with a small pile of cash.

My mother came with me to the interview. She was more than happy to lie for me and say that I was 16. The camp director, a pious, nervous Jewish man, hired me on the spot. I seemed like such a nice Jewish girl, and my Holocaust Survivor mother touched his Jewish heart.

What none of us knew, at that moment, was that it would turn out to be one of the worst decisions of my life. First, I didn't really like children, with whom I had never before had much luck with; and, second, there were very few women on staff and, holy Christ, there were so many men, so many men, and so many of those men wanted me at a time in my life when I didn't turn anyone down.

❧ Dancing with Frankie ☙

⌘

My fantasy of a smooth, classy resort with pleasant accommodations and great food crashed into the reality of a down-at-the-heels hotel in Loch Sheldrake that hadn't been renovated since its heyday in the early 1960s. The Evans Hotel looked nice enough when you drove up, but counselors were warned to make themselves scarce out front, and were strictly forbidden from entering the lobby or mingling with guests. Our quarters were located out back, inside a row of dilapidated, multi-roomed hovels with mildewed doorjambs and water-stained ceilings. They looked more like rotting cardboard boxes than cabins. Three iron cots were stuffed into each eight by eight room, and everyone lived out of their suitcases.

But at night, there were small gatherings, and I quickly fell in with the hippies who assembled in one of the boys' bunks. There was pot smoking but nothing and no one sufficiently interesting to keep my interest. No sex, no politics, no art, just stoner babble. I ended up talking mainly to one boy and kissed him too, but he started acting like we were boyfriend and girlfriend. So I dropped back, and avoided him. When he found out a few days later that the reason I hadn't visited one night was because I went to bed with another boy, he confronted me, angry and hurt.

He was a nice boy and I didn't want to hurt his feelings. But, my feelings were pretty much summed up in one of my favorite folk songs of the day – "that's what you get for loving me." If he confused kisses for commitment, he got it wrong. I was a wild seed and I knew it. If a boy didn't know it, he wasn't paying attention. Not my fault.

The boy I'd spent that evening with was a religious Jew who wore a white silk yarmulke I'd noticed when it streaked past me one day in the hot summer sun. He was very handsome and, to my amazement, he was British. But it was the yarmulke that got me, or rather the idea that someone actually believed in the things represented by the yarmulke. I'd never socialized with religious Jews. They intrigued me. They were as alien to me as Catholics and Christians, curious throwbacks who believed in magical things, and yet they were somehow profoundly connected to me through blood and tradition. I felt an incredible urge to sleep with him.

The next day, I waylaid him and started a conversation with him. He quickly invited me to come to his room that night. I accepted and, according to his wishes, didn't tell anyone and took a circuitous route to get there, sneaking around the hotel and hoping none of the guests saw me through the windows. He had a better job than the rest of us, so his room was inside the hotel. It was a proper room with proper furniture and a double bed, and a cheap lamp on a bedside table. It felt luxurious.

We lay on the bed to talk, him in a dark wool suit and a crisp white shirt and the silk yarmulke, me in shorts, sandals and a tee. He pressed his crotch into my hand.

We kissed and he stopped it; then he kissed me again and stopped again. He begged for stimulation but within moments of providing it, he pushed me away. At each interval, he fell into a pit of despair, claiming we were sinning. He blamed me, as if I was the Jezebel and he my helpless victim, making me so irritated, I'd want to leave. Then he'd beg me to stay, and touch me or kiss me and repeat the cycle again and again.

Very little actually happened in that bed but by morning, it felt as if I'd had a hundred terrible sexual experiences. I felt traumatized by his constant criticisms and came to believe that he was right, the whole experience was my fault. I couldn't deny that in the back of my mind I had wanted the thrill of corrupting a religious man. It was precisely his religiosity that made me want to see his cock. But now some of his guilt had washed into me, and I felt like the horrible person he'd made me out to be.

Something strange was happening to me. I was losing my sense of self. Things were slipping beyond my control. Things were, in fact, spiraling out of control. I was getting sucked into other people's madness. I was playing roles I didn't want to play, doing things that didn't feel real. Men were so much crazier than I could ever have believed. My father was the nicest man in the world. But none of the men I'd met were anything like him. They all wanted things from me, things I didn't have to give, things I didn't want to give. All I wanted was the happy joy of companionship and affectionate sex.

People were complicated. I was complicated too but not like them. I didn't understand their morals and they didn't understand mine. I didn't see where or how I would ever fit in. For example, I knew that most girls like children and dreamt of growing up and having them. Not me. I never spent time with children, I never ever dreamt of having my own, and by the end of the first day, while other girls busily bonded with their wards, I loathed the job.

Instead of that group of eager learners to guide, I was given a group of pre-schoolers. Toddlers are, of course, completely insane. They wander, they drift, they run for no reason, they sit down and can't be moved, they throw tantrums, they cling to your leg, and sometimes, they leak from both ends. They are so adorable and darling you simply want to love them, until they throw up on you or otherwise degrade you with their body fluids. When they are unhappy, the sounds they emit vibrate so deeply into your core you think your brain will split. I loved them but I could not stand being near them for more than an hour at a time.

Even as a babysitter, the kids I minded were obedient school-aged kids. I had no experience of four-year-olds, nor any idea what to expect. The more time I spent with them, the more disgusting I found them. They dripped, they drooled, they quarreled and bit each other, and then they crawled into your arms all grubby and wet with fresh tears to babble incoherently about nonsensical things. Yes, they looked like angels and I cuddled them. I couldn't help it, they were so cute. But I had seen the most angelic of the lot, a tiny princess of a girl whom I'd doted on until that day, lean over the lunch table and sadistically squash a fly into the butter dish. Honestly, they frightened me.

I also had a more gnawing concern. I'd forgotten my vibrator at home and I couldn't find any place private enough to jerk off. Going without orgasms was just...impossible. I needed the relief too much. After a few lackluster attempts, I found a two-pronged solution in my second week there.

I noticed there was a lot of slack time during lunch, and that it took forever to shuttle the kids back out. So after seating the kids, I'd duck out and let my co-counselor deal with supervising them. It was sleazy, I knew, but she didn't seem to mind. I'd dart back to my room and lock the door, then rifle through one of my roomies' suitcases. She'd lent me her electric shaver to do my legs so I knew where it was. I left my panties on to avoid getting hair trapped and buzzed myself off to pillow-biting orgasm. I'd wipe any telltale juices off the shaver, put it back in her bag, and return to the dining hall in time to meet the kids as they came out the door.

A few days into this new routine, I passed out after my orgasm. By the time I woke up, it was late afternoon. I went to find the kids, but they were all gone and I found out that other counselors had to help shepherd them to their parents. I felt bad about that, but also relieved that I did not have to wipe another snotty nose or clasp another sticky little hand that day. Plus it was Friday – and this meant an early start on the Friday night revelry.

The hotel was going to be filled to the brim this weekend, because Frankie Avalon would be performing. It was half cool, half ridiculous. He was a quaint oddity, a cheesy old guy who I associated with Annette Funicello and beach blanket movies. Still, he was the most famous Hollywood star I'd ever had a chance to meet and it was fun to see people running around, trying to spruce up the hotel for the influx of guests from other hotels.

My plans were almost thwarted when, without warning, two boys from my parents' neighborhood, one of them my neighbor, Rob, showed up suddenly in a car they drove all the way from Brooklyn. Someone who heard it from someone else said there were boys waiting for me by the hotel entrance. I hurried out there and Rob was sitting in his old beater, waving at me to get in the car with them. Rob tried to convince me that, after he drove all that way, I owed it to him now to take off with him and his friend.

I was speechless. We'd gone on one date. One. I had turned him down for a repeat. Rob was sweet but also very introverted and weird. How did he know where I was? I hadn't told him. Had he been spying on me? Tapping my phones?

My mother solved that mystery a few months later: in my absence, he'd started dropping by almost daily to talk to her about me. She found his obsession charming and kept him coming back by updating him whenever I sent a letter. She'd let him know I was working in Loch Sheldrake at the Evans Hotel.

I could feel the stares of some counselors on my back as I stood on the road, talking to the boys. They'd heard the announcement on the PA system, and came to gawk. I stuck to my guns, and said I couldn't leave my job, and that he needed to go back to Brooklyn. I ran back to the hotel feeling shaken and insecure. A small crowd of gossipers stared accusingly at me, as if I'd actually had sex with the boys I'd talked to on the road. I decided to stay in that night, with the door locked. If Rob drove all that way, would he really just turn around and leave, or would he come back angry or violent? I had no idea. His behavior made no sense to me. Its irrationality scared me.

It was only my second weekend at the hotel, but those two weeks had been mind-bending, mind-numbing, and surreal. It seemed that everywhere I went, there was another boy who wanted to be intimate with me. Some of the girls I worked with stopped talking to me, but I was too self-absorbed to notice their resentment or to worry that my sex life had become grist for the employee rumor mill. In reality, I hadn't even removed all my clothes with anyone but in the small world of hotel employees, my free-loving ways tarred me as a whore. I felt dirty inside and out, without redemption, and yet freer in some ways because I couldn't sink any lower. On one level, I didn't care what small-minded straights thought. On another, I swam in their sea and socialized in their world. I didn't want to be ostracized.

Saturday night was my last chance to see Frankie Avalon, and then to my disappointment, we weren't allowed in to his performance. Instead, my two roommates and I assembled at the after-party, where he was dancing and drinking with his band. We grabbed a table and gaped at him from the sidelines, making snarky comments about his processed hair and polyester clothes.

On impulse, I jumped to my feet, and told my friends I was going to dance with him. I went on the dance floor, sidled up beside him and asked for a dance. To my joy, he accepted and we danced. He was very relaxed and friendly, and I got comforta-ble right away. He asked my age, and when I told him 15, al-most 16, he began making odd, almost apologetic comments about not being able to sleep with me and how he was married with kids.

It hit me bitterly and strangely. WTF? I didn't want to sleep with him. Why in the world did he think that I did? I danced with him on a lark, so I could laugh about it with friends and go home with a little of his Hollywood fairy dust on my sleeve. Now he was acting as if I was a temptress trying to lure him to adultery. What the fucking fuck was wrong with him? Or was it me? What the fucking fuck was wrong with me? Because I probably **would** have slept with him if he asked, certain that it would make a great story I could write about some day.

He spun me around in his arms, holding me tight, his face close to mine. He was old and wrinkly but he was supremely fit, and I thought, oh my God, I'm going to end up in his room. That would be too weird and too funny all at the same time. And...his hair...it is so...stiff! How did he have sex with that hair? How did he even get it that stiff?

He danced me over to his drummer, introducing him as Chuck Stevens, the brother of songstress Connie Stevens, and released me from his arms.

"Chuck, take this kid out," Frankie said. "Feed her a nice steak, ok?" Frankie looked into my eyes. "You go with the drummer, he'll get you a steak."

What? Had he sensed my sexuality or my hunger? No matter, FREE STEAK DINNER! I promptly asked if my friends could come. Frankie nodded so I grabbed my roomies and off we went with the drummer and a silent chauffeur who drove us to a late night restaurant in South Fallsburg.

Now, the whole time I'd been at the Evans, I probably hadn't eaten a single solid meal. It was hard to eat with the children because their table manners were so nauseating, and counselors were left to fend for ourselves for dinners. For kids with driver's licenses, that meant scooting into town for cheap eats. For me, this meant going to smoke pot and hoping someone brought food back to pass around. But I never minded going hungry, and skipping meals was second nature to me.

Mr. Stevens, I could tell, was summing me up and reaching the conclusion that I was destined for trouble and in dire need of a good meal. So he and the silent driver smiled indulgently as they watched us wolf down steak and bread and potatoes like it was the first meal we'd had all year. I'm not saying it was a great steak but to me that night it was prime, and the sheer excitement of it all – being in a brightly lit restaurant on a Saturday night, eating a steak dinner with a famous musician – made me chatter brightly.

At meal's end, they paid and drove us back to the hotel and told us to stay out of trouble. I was relieved because for a few minutes there, I thought Frankie had assigned me to have sex with Mr. Stevens, but it was nothing like that. I still think fondly of the mildly freaked-out look on Mr. Stevens' kind face as he babysat me that night.

When I woke the next day, my roomies had left on a shopping trip in a nearby town. I stayed in bed, still exhilarated. I had touched the aura of a dream. Had a little of its glitter fallen on me? I wanted to relive the evening again and again, especially the moments Frankie expertly swirled me around the floor, his trained body fluid and strong as he carried me along. I couldn't stop giggling that it was the man from the beach blanket movies, and how did a hippie like me even parse his processed hairdo, but that didn't diminish its romance. I relived the steak dinner too, imagining that my girlish gabbling was the sparkling conversation I'd so often dreamt I'd have some day with famous men. I spent the day jerking off again and again with the purloined electric razor, totally happy for the first time since I'd arrived.

The next morning, I was called into the office of the pious man who had met my mother and believed our story that I was a good Jewish girl. The counselors who had been picking up my slack did not share my shallow indifference to the children's welfare. The rumor mill had churned out shocking tales of my immorality.

The pious man was horrified. What kind of female neglects children? What manner of perversion had he allowed into his camp? I was fired. He wanted me off the premises the next day.

❧ The Gilbert ☙ Grand Guignol

⌘

I could not go home. I would not. I couldn't return in shame, in failure, fired because I was a bad person. I could not tell my parents what happened or why. My mother would never let me live it down. It would only add to her emotionally crippling ammunition. I could not go home.

Someone told someone who told me that they were looking for help at a hotel not too far away, The Gilbert Hotel. Someone else volunteered someone to drive me there to apply. Thanks to that series of someones, before the day was out, I'd been interviewed by the middle aged bleached blonde who ran the place and hired on the spot to become their night shift switchboard operator. I didn't know how to run a switchboard, so I inflated my skills with office equipment and said I was a fast learner, and she wearily said not to worry, I'd be trained. They needed a body and I was the body that walked through the door before anyone else. Since I'd already been working at the Evans, she took my word that I was 16, and I left the Gilbert's with a profound sense of salvation and grace.

I had a new job. I would have an income that didn't depend on tips. $40 a week. I was rich! I could tell my parents that I simply took a better, better-paying job. They'd never know the truth.

After the Evans, the Gilbert seemed upscale. Staff was housed in a big flimsy firetrap with rickety stairs but it was cleaner and far better built than the last place. I was on the third floor, and the room had big window with a pretty view. The room was nice and neat, with 2 real beds and dressers. My roommate was a counselor, and since she worked by day and I worked by night, we never saw each other. Both male and female staff resided in the building, giving it the feel of a dorm, with parties going on at all hours of the day and night and rock music echoing down the halls at all times.

Working the switchboard made me part of the adult hotel staff. They let me eat in the main dining room with the musicians and senior waiters, walk the interior halls freely, and socialize with whomever I liked. Working the night shift seemed like the coolest thing of all. I always felt most alive at night. The most interesting things happened then.

The switchboard was a fantastic machine. I gasped when I saw it, awed that they were giving me full control over it for the night. It was a PBX 555 with scores of colorful cords hanging out and a gigantic panel of holes, each one marked for a room or a hotel service. True to my word, I learned how to operate it in record time. It was a grown-up job, and a genuine challenge. I fell in love with that big funky switchboard, and felt like a queen of the night sitting in the swivel chair with my headphones on, connecting conversations after midnight. When I closed my eyes to sleep the next day, I'd still see the plugs going into the holes.

Most of the late night callers were grumpy guests seeking services or complaining about a burned out light bulb or insufficient towels, but some of them – as I quickly learned – were horny people trying to set up trysts. I always felt a thrill when I connected them, occasionally eavesdropping on the brief, urgent conversations arranging which room to meet in. One night, everyone seemed agitated, and calls were coming and going from a particular room. I listened in to find out that a guest had died in that room. A secret operation was underway to remove the corpse and escort the widow away from the hotel without any of the other guests noticing, because the owner was afraid it would spook them. They had a plan in place to remove the body by back-routes. It was eerie but felt very important that night to connect all the people involved in this grim duty.

The switchboard was just off the main lobby, so I could see people coming and going from the bar, where the entertainment ranged from lounge singers to strippers on weekends. There were a lot of lonely wives in the hotel, but they seemed to live for the swimming pool and tanning, and only an occasional mink stole would wander by to hit the bar. On the other hand, men were constantly coming and going in the lobby, especially the staff, who did the work that guests never saw. Once in a while, the boss dropped by too. He was the brother of the blonde who'd hired me, a taciturn man with a kind of bony, ghoulish aspect like Raymond Massey, but he was always very friendly, and seemed to approve of the job I was doing.

I'd learned my lesson: I was always prompt and seldom left my desk. It was so perfect for me to be left alone with this huge novel machine, and I threw myself into memorizing its numbers and mastering it so I could connect and disconnect fast. Meanwhile, more and more men seemed to be dropping by for casual late night chatter. I was a captive audience for all the insomniac men on staff. The friendliest of the lot was the guy in charge of the hotel's massive maintenance staff, from maids to plumbers. His name was Lars, he was Scandinavian by birth but lived in a local Catskills town.

Lars was sweet and shy and obese. He had a walrus moustache and a pageboy haircut, which reminded me of Captain Kangaroo. He was about fifteen years older than me too, but he was kind, and dropped by every night with a snack for me and would talk to me earnestly, sincerely, from the depths of his being. He told me about how lonely he was, how unhappy he'd felt his whole life. Meeting me had changed everything. Now at last he saw a bright future, with me in it.

I didn't take him seriously. How could I? He didn't know who he was talking to. I wasn't the angel he thought he loved. I was the girl who got kicked out of a hotel for being depraved. The more I tried to discourage him, the more I tried to tell him that I was not a good person on the inside, and that getting involved with me was a mistake, the harder he fell. He was wearing me down. I began wondering if he would be such a bad choice after all. He was so damn sincere, so in love with me. Why would I push away someone so in love with me? Love mattered more than looks, didn't it?

Finally, he convinced me to go out for a cocktail with him. I'd never had a cocktail. Just the word cocktail made me giddy. It had cock in it. But it was also so sophisticated, so very Jackie O. I wanted a cocktail. So I went.

He drove me to a bar far from the hotel, and when we sat down, he ordered me something called a "seven and seven." I knew it was illegal for me to be in a bar. That added to its glamour. The cocktail didn't taste great but it tasted like adulthood, so I drank deep. Lars again explained his fantasy to me, now at greater length. It was a long and complicated story about how difficult it would be for us, how much we had to overcome, but how, in the end, we would find a way, as true love always does.

"I'm sure my wife will understand," he said. "I know how to explain it to her, I'm sure she'll understand."

I couldn't believe it. I didn't want another woman's man. I was only hanging out with him because he seemed so lonely and so needy, and was so friendly to me. He never told me he was married. Married! Yuck! Why wasn't he spending time with his wife?

I avoided him after that. When he dropped by the switchboard, I acted too busy to talk. Now that he'd admitted he was married, he knew the jig was up with me: he seemed embarrassed and kept insisting we could work it out but finally gave up. PHEW! Dodged another bullet, I thought. At least no one got hurt, I thought.

I was walking to work across the hotel's big campus a few days after the doomed drink when, out of the blue, a young foreign woman with a child in her arms came rushing up to me, her face streaked by tears. Lars was running behind her, panting.

"Don't take my husband!" she cried. She held the baby out to me. "We have a baby! Leave my husband alone, we have a baby!" Lars finally reached us, sweat dripping from his moustache. He engulfed the mother and child under his massive arm and walked them away.

"I'm sorry," he called over his shoulder. "I'm so sorry, Gloria."

"I don't want your husband," I shouted to her wildly. "I don't want him!" I took off running, not stopping until I was behind my switchboard, alone and safe behind the impassive machine.

❧ Flirting ❧
As Fast As I Could

⌘

That was it. I had it with straight, so-called normal guys. My next male friend was a Communist named Arlen. He was very short and very hairy, with a thick and stubby cock, and, like Leon, he let me do what I wanted to him, without pushing for more or complaining. He was sweet, loyal, easy to spend time with, and a very smart college boy at an Ivy League school, but he could not stop talking about Communism. While I was a leftie myself, I always rejected Communism, and we'd end up quarreling about it. Similarly, while I'm not a Zionist his own anti-Zionism was so virulent that it made me wonder if he was a self-hating Jew. He was an American Jew, I thought, he could not possibly understand how the child of a Holocaust survivor felt about more Jews dying. I had to go.

Since the staff housing was co-ed, there was no shortage of men and boys. I'd usually wake up in the afternoon, when most of the waiters and busboys were between shifts and the odor of pot wafted through the halls. I'd dog that sweet stink until I found its source, and let myself be lured into rooms where I'd end up making out, sucking off, giving handjobs to, and otherwise having low-key no-strings-attached teen sex. Now and again a boy would start to get serious about me, wanting me to spend all my time with him. I would stop seeing him and focus on someone else.

There was always someone else, always. There was always another bed, another room, another man, another adventure to be had. I went everywhere I could. I wanted to see EVERYTHING, from the grungy basements to the glitzy dining rooms. I liked laborers as much as rich guys. I was simply amazed that so many of them wanted to be with me. I said yes and yes and yes.

I was beginning to realize that, although I didn't want it, although I never asked for it, I had some kind of weird and creepy sexual power over men. I couldn't understand why it was but it was. At the same time, I knew most of them didn't really like me, they just liked me enough to have sex with me. Maybe it was my big breasts or my big brain, maybe I was in the right place at the wrong time or the wrong place at the right time, but whatever it was, it confused the hell out of me.

It confused partners too. I seemed easygoing and uninhibited at first come on, but when we got down to it, I needed to be in charge. I preferred keeping as much of my own clothes on as possible, and didn't want anyone spending too much time near my pussy. I much preferred doing to being done, and pushed back men who got too aggressive in bed. I wanted them to be naked and vulnerable, not me.

Though I was trying to stick with hippie-type boys, straight ones were still flying under the radar into my lust zone. I had a repeat of yarmulke guy only this time it was a fair-haired, blue-eyed, peach fuzzy Baptist who lived a floor above me. Different religion, smaller penis, same humiliating experience: he would initiate, then stop me and blame me for turning him on, then initiate and say something else unkind, yet when I'd try to leave, he'd get doe-eyed and apologetic. I could not tear myself away, falling once more into the conviction that I was a bad person.

The rollercoaster of my adolescent hormonal storm shifted into high gear. One minute I was exhilarated by all the new experiences flooding into my consciousness but an hour later I felt depressed and ashamed of the things I'd done. With every passing summer day, the world was drifting away from me. More and more, I felt like a voyeur and witness of my life than someone who was living it. I saw myself go with boys and I thought about it remotely, critically, as if watching myself in a movie. The only time I felt real was behind the switchboard, alone with my cords and plugs and the machine between me and the world.

I don't know if I gained any notoriety for my relaxed attitude to relationships but even if I did, the Gilbert management took a laissez-faire approach to amorous antics. One of the best-loved people at the hotel was the handsome social director, an Italian guy with a deep tan, thick hair, white teeth, and the voracious libido required to service lonely summer widows starving for sex. His name was Tommy Carter of Westport (though, as he privately revealed, really Tony Carpucci from Bay Ridge) and from the first time I saw him running bingo at the pool, I wanted him. He was definitely an off-brand: sort of straight, late 30s, but there was something entirely adorable and charming about him and no doubt in my mind he was a party animal of the finest kind, a true hedonist. He was the hotel's in-house celebrity, and he played to the crowd with funny hats and endless jokes. He was a true Italian stallion, exuding testosterone at the perfect level to keep ladies smiling.

I remember the summer wives, playing mahjong and sunning themselves to take the edge off their malcontent. One 40-something brunette with heavy make-up was notorious for her habit of rubbing her own nipple in public. She'd come to the lobby dressed to the nines, in blue chiffon and sparkly earrings, and stand to the side, holding her breast in one hand as she teased her nipple through her dress. Sometimes she'd reach inside her bikini top and do it at the pool. Staff whispered about it and occasionally spied on her from a discreet distance, but no one stopped her or suggested she take her hobby to her room. We all quiescently accepted that, as a paying guest, she had the right to stimulate her nipple wherever she liked.

It didn't take long for Tommy to notice me. I showed up at the pool a couple of times, then he dropped by the switchboard, and then he invited me to go out with a group of people to see the show at another hotel. I was so pleased. Another new experience to notch on my belt!

The car ride over was strange but interesting. The men were more or less my father's age, only wilder, more profane, and clearly mobbed up. I'd grown up around kids whose uncles and fathers worked for the Mafia so this kind of relaxed me. The other woman in the car wore a mink stole and sipped a martini the whole way there. She was unexpectedly friendly to me, and offered me cigarettes and a slug from a bottle she had in her purse. She conversed with me in a raspy, whiskey voice, then stared out the window when I told her my age. I don't remember much else, except that everyone was nice to me and after a couple of hours we came home, and it all felt magnificently and soothingly calm and adult to me.

A few days later, Tommy invited me to party with him in the nightclub. They had a special act lined up for the weekend late night show. I was covering two shifts that Saturday, and the boss said I could take a full hour off between shifts to freshen up and eat while someone covered the switchboard for me. Tommy said that would be a perfect time to drop by, so as soon as I could, I changed into a glittery shirt in the bathroom and arrived at the club with the late night show already in progress.

I glanced inside. The room was filled almost entirely with men who were frozen with delight, mouths gaping, cigars held midair, eyes fixed at the stage. Then I saw why. Sparkles flew and sheer sails floated to reveal a near-naked full-bodied female swirling and wriggling. It was a strip show. I'd heard of them but never seen one. Holy shit, I was in the belly of the patriarchy! I didn't think I had the guts to go into the room but I was dying to get a front row seat for this show.

Tommy spotted me and waved at me to come in and sit with him. I tiptoed to his table and drank whatever he ordered for me as I watched. The dancer slithered and shimmied and swayed in ways I never saw anyone move before, a brilliant smile painted on her face. Curve after creamy curve of ripe flesh appeared and vanished as she hypnotized the men. The men grossed me out. The whole thing was hideously uncool and sexist. On the other hand, she was so gorgeous and most of the men in the room were toads. They were her drooling fools. I watched her face. She didn't give a shit about them. She was working her act. It took a lot of concentration to maintain that smile while she swung her hips all over the room.

Tommy was the MC, so every now and again, he'd throw jokes her way or egg the crowd on to applaud. I didn't know whether to leave or stay. The feminist in me was angry but the horny teen in me was titillated. So I stayed until she finished her act, and snuck out as the audience was finishing its ovation.

The next time Tommy invited me out he invited me in, into his room. His room was off by itself, behind the dinner club, and it was much nicer than any of the others, even nicer than the guest rooms. The room had been his summer home for many years and he personalized it with cozy linens and pillows, and a nice chair. Most of the floor space was taken up by a king-sized bed, a rarity in those days. Naturally, once I got to his room, the bed was where we sat to talk, and where the talk turned into sex.

I was crazy about Tommy, not in a serious in-love way but in a light and cheery one. When I told him I didn't want to fuck, he shrugged. He didn't want to fuck either. He tried to save that for a girlfriend back home. He seemed honest and caring, and he focused on my pleasure. No one had ever made my pleasure a priority. Nor had anyone been able to get me so wet and orgasmic! It felt so different when he touched my pussy. He had huge hands, like a butcher, yet his fingers were magically soft, patient, persistent, and intuitive. Within seconds, he would have me purring and curling up to him and writhing in lust. He was sexy on the receiving end too, but his ability to bring me to orgasms with his fingers was the most wonderful thing that had ever happened to me.

Didn't this feel good, he'd ask, gently massaging my clit? Oh God yes, it felt good, it felt better than anything a man had ever done to me before, oh yes. How about when he pushed his finger inside? Oh yes, yes, yes, yes.

There was no need to discuss discretion. He had his reputation as a gigolo to protect and I didn't want my peers to know that I was making it with an aging Guido/Sinatra wannabe who held the finger to my heart.

Instead, we met when we could, as we could, and enjoyed our time together without either hiding that we were friends or revealing that we were lovers. I could have gone on all summer long like that, working the switchboard and getting finger-fucked and kissed by Tommy while enjoying casual dalliances with boys closer to my own age.

I was happy secretly crushing on Tommy's muscular, hairy body, his thick cock, his warm smile, and his amazing middle finger. I couldn't wait to ride his finger as often as I could. About two weeks into it, I snuck into his room, knowing he'd be returning from the pool soon, and stripped naked to wait for him. He didn't look nearly as happy as I expected him to be when he found me there. He relaxed after a while but it was too late; I felt a dark foreboding that I'd overstepped a boundary with him.

A few days later, he asked if I'd like to meet a close friend of his. He thought the two of us would hit it off great. His friend was even classier and more successful than he was, a real, good looking Frank Sinatra type, Tommy told me. He was the social director at Grossinger's. He'd met Jerry Lewis and hundreds of celebrities. He was sophisticated and savvy but, at heart, a salt of the earth Brooklyn boy. No pressure, he assured me, but he thought I'd love this guy.

Was I willing to meet?

Of course I was. Yes.

❧ The Dark Wing of Fear ☙

⌘

I met him.

Johnny looked and talked more like a made man than a social director. Maybe he was both. He wore an expensive double-breasted navy sports coat and a fine silk ascot to hide his wrinkled neck. All that was missing was the yachting cap. Like Tommy, Johnny had a full head of thick black hair and a mouth full of bright white teeth, but he was shorter and barrel-chested, and not as smart. He looked more like Paulie Walnuts than Frank Sinatra, down to the carefully combed wave in the hair, and was closer to 50 than to 40. But admittedly he had style, even though it was not a style I ever went for.

"Johnny's going to take you for dinner and a show at his hotel," Tommy said enthusiastically. "You're going to love it."

We sat in Tommy's room to talk. A small poodle was prancing around. Tommy was minding it for the girlfriend back home, and Johnny was playing with it and calling it by name. He made some crude jokes about how horny the poodle was and began to flip and rub its penis shaft, half-joking about jerking it off.

I was frozen in shock. The idea of touching an animal's genitals was beyond my ken. The men were laughing, and Tommy told him to knock it off, acting like it was a harmless joke. Perhaps. I didn't want to judge but it freaked me out, and I made up my mind that I didn't want to be alone with this poodle-molesting mafia dude.

We went to the bar, and things got more normal. Johnny was gracious and warm, and made me have a cocktail with him. Finally, he said it was time to get going if we wanted to make the show at his hotel. I wasn't so sure about leaving with him, and turned to Tommy, questioningly. I just didn't know. Johnny didn't feel as safe as Tommy. Tommy put his arm around me.

"You don't have to go if you don't want to," he said. "But you should, because you'll have fun."

"I'll take good care of you," Johnny said. They stood on either side of me, smiling. They were so familiar to me, these two aging Brooklyn boys who'd made good in the Catskills, and, like me, loved guilt-free, hedonistic adventures. Oh hell. What was the worst that could happen – a dull evening with a cheesy old guy eating a great meal and seeing a genuine kitschy Catskills show for free?

"Sure," I said, and with that one word of consent, the adventure began.

When we drove to Grossinger's, Johnny turned up the charm. He was convivial and gallant, and when we got to the hotel, the maitre d' rushed up to him as if he was a celebrity, and showed us to one of the best tables in the house. The room was drenched with lights, tables crowded by wealthy people in furs and jewels and suits. On stage, a pumped-up brass band was hammering it. My head swam in the manic energy that exploded from every corner.

Johnny was in his element now. He ordered drinks for us with authority, commanding eager underlings. Throughout the room, perfumed hands waved to Johnny and he waved back with feigned indifference. He knew everyone. Men would sidle up to the table, shouting, "You're the man, Johnny!" When the bandleader took the mike to announce that Johnny was in the room, everyone stopped moving and a drum rolled as a spotlight fell on our table. Johnny grabbed my arm and made me stand up with him. The room applauded loudly, and he gave me an uncomfortably tight hug.

"This is my new girl," he announced grandly, as I died a thousand deaths of embarrassment. I wasn't his girl! What the fuck. He was showing me off in a super-creepy way, as if to say, "Yeah, an old fuck like me got this big-titted young chick, ha!"

What a mistake. Why did I go on a date with a known poodle molester? Yuck! People were bowing and scraping and he was eating it up. This wasn't glamorous, it was sad. I had the alienating feeling that he and I were not even on the same date. I was there to have a pleasant evening and he was acting like he owned me. Creepy bourgeois fucker. He was so busy sucking up flattery that he'd never ordered the dinner I was hoping for.

"When are we going to eat?" I asked. He'd ordered several rounds of drinks by now, but no menus had appeared. I was starving.

"Oh no, we missed dinner a long time ago, this is just drinks." My face fell. "Don't worry, I'll put some food in you. Here," he signaled a passing busboy, "you! Get her a bread basket from the kitchen and bring me another round." He leaned in and said, "I'll take you to an Italian restaurant later tonight. You'll like it."

I didn't want there to be a later tonight. I wanted to go back to the hotel, and said so. I ate a roll while he downed his drink and finally, FINALLY, he said we could leave. As we got into his car, I saw him stagger a little. Perfect. He was drunk, I thought. Now I could stop worrying about going hungry and start worrying about dying in a car crash. I curled into a ball of anxiety on the seat beside him as he veered along the road, sipping from the cocktail he carried out of the hotel and pontificating drunkenly.

The car pulled to a stop in front of a small motel.

"What's this?" I peered out, thinking he'd taken me to the restaurant anyway.

"I need to get something from my room," he said. "Come on. It'll take a minute. I don't want to leave you sitting outside alone."

I sighed impatiently. It looked deserted but there were lights on in a few of the rooms, so I got out of the car and followed him through a series of corridors until we came to a small suite of rooms. He went to his bed and sat down, fiddling with something in his nightstand drawer.

"Come here," he said.

I walked over, thinking he wanted to show me what was in the drawer.

He grabbed me hard. He pushed me hard onto the floor, pressing my shoulders down until I was on my knees. I couldn't fight him; seated at the edge of the bed, the power of his massive chest behind him, his arms were steel.

He held me with one hand and unzipped his fly.

"Suck me off," he said.

"No, I don't want to."

He forced my mouth to his cock and I sealed my lips. He took a bottle of pills from the drawer.

"Take these," he said. "I want you to take some of these."

"No!" There was no way I was taking unknown pills from him.

"Take them!" He shook me hard.

"No fucking way," I said.

"I'll kill you," he said. "I'll fuck you up. You'll never walk again. Suck my dick."

"What are you saying?!" I cried in fear.

My brain was spinning. He was a rapist and he was drunk. He was a drunk rapist who was going to drug me and kill me. He couldn't kill me in his room, could he? People would hear, wouldn't they? What was I going to do? Why the fuck had I agreed to go with him? Fuck, fuck, fuck.

"Suck me," he said. He forced his cock into my mouth. I struggled to pull away.

"You bitch," he said. "I'll fucking kill you, you bitch, I'll shoot you. Suck me."

I did. He came and he shot his cum down my throat, threatening and cursing the whole time. He only let me go when he was spent.

I cringed on the floor in a state of shock.

"OK," he said, "let's get some food." He stood up from the bed, zipped up and adjusted his belt as if nothing unusual had happened. "What are you waiting for, come on, I'll take you to a good Italian place. You'll love it."

I couldn't move.

"Oh, come on, don't be like that, you'll like the place, you're hungry right?"

I got to my feet and followed him out. I don't know what I was thinking. I wasn't thinking. My brain was numb. I got in the car and we went to the restaurant. It was a mom and pop type place. A fat cheerful lady welcomed us. She knew Johnny and immediately scurried around to serve him, treating him like a long-lost brother, telling me how lucky I was to be with such an important man.

I don't remember if we talked or what we talked about. I don't remember the food or how I endured the meal, while Johnny kept acting as if nothing unusual had happened while I was still in a state of terror and violent disgust. I could still taste his sperm in my throat and it tasted like bile. It felt like I'd never be able to get that taste out of my mouth.

Johnny paid the bill and we walked back to the car. All I wanted was to get back to the hotel, to my room, to my safety. All I wanted was to get as far away from his evil as I possibly could. But there was still the ride home. I was on alert the whole way, keeping one hand on the door handle, ready to jump if I had to.

We were on the highway when Johnny took a surprise turn and drove me along a dirt road. There were no houses, no hotels, no lights, just deep woods on either side. He slowed the vehicle to a stop.

"Suck me off," he said. "You owe me for the meal. It was good, wasn't it?"

For the next ten minutes, I begged, pleaded, and bargained with him. Woods equaled death, I thought. Even if I jumped out here, how far would I get in the middle of the night by myself? If he caught me, he'd kill me and leave me for dead, just another gruesome statistic, a bunch of scattered remains that a hunter would find one day.

Just drive me close to the hotel, I nagged. No, I promise I wouldn't go in. I wouldn't. How about just driving me close enough to see the lights? As long as I saw lights, I'd feel better. I was scared of the dark. I was scared of the woods. I couldn't do it there. I'd suck him off better this time, better than I ever sucked off anyone, just let me see some lights and then I'd calm down and do whatever he wanted me to do, I promised, I swore, I wouldn't lie, I'd do anything he wanted, just let me see the hotel's lights.

My life started over when he reluctantly gave in. There was hope.

As he drove, he made me promise again and again that I would do what he wanted and not run away and made me tell him that I liked him and wanted to be with him, and that he was wonderful and that I really wanted to suck his cock.

He turned back onto a highway and a few minutes later, I saw the Gilbert front lights glimmering about a quarter of a mile away. Johnny pulled onto the shoulder.

"Close enough," he said, slowing the car to a stop.

"Yes," I said, pulling the door handle. I bolted from the car, running as fast as I could towards the light.

"Motherfucker! Bitch! Get back here! Cocksucking bitch!"

He drove on the shoulder, the door still gaping open, as if trying to scoop me back on the side. I turned and darted straight towards the side lobby, climbing over the fence to spring across the long manicured lawn separating the road from the hotel. I didn't want to look back, but I did, and I saw his headlights still advancing slowly towards the entrance of the hotel.

God how I ran. I ran and ran and ran, until I ran through a hotel door.

I was numb and dizzy and changed in ways I didn't know. I sat down on a vinyl chair and tried to cry but the tears wouldn't come.

✂ My Private Vietnam ✂

⌘

What was wrong with me? How stupid was I? Was it rape or was it what I deserved? Johnny saw me as a whore – why? Because I dressed sexy and had big tits and acted so free about sex? Well, wasn't that what a whore was? If I was a whore, ok, but did I have to be a stupid whore? The taste of his sperm would never go away. If I threw up a thousand times, I'd still taste it. I was such an idiot, a disgusting whorish idiot.

A slim guy with a crew cut walked through the door. He was exceptionally neat and clean, which made sense when he told me he was a GI. It was very late, and he was surprised to find a young girl sitting alone, looking so upset. He sat down and asked me what happened. I told him. Not down to all the details I'm recounting here, but I told him about the ugly, fearful episodes, and how I'd escaped and ended up here, and now I was too overwhelmed to move. What if Johnny was still out there, waiting for me?

Army boy sat with me for an hour. His presence was comforting. He told me he was between tours of duty, earning a little scratch at the hotel. He said he felt bad for me. The feeling was mutual when he sighed that he was shipping back to Vietnam in a few days. That was worse than being raped, I thought. We sat quietly, feeling bad for each other and ourselves.

"Give me a handjob before you go," he said, thrusting himself on me and pressing me back on the orange vinyl chair. "Just give me a handjob," he whispered, "you can do it, you just did worse."

I tried to pull away but he too held me tight, whispering, "Just a handjob, come on, don't make me hurt you."

I couldn't believe what was happening. I didn't understand how he could do this to me after hearing what I'd just been through. I tried to escape but it was hopeless.

For the second time that night, a man had me pinned.

He got his cock out of his pants and forced my hand around it.

"Yeah, like that, do it, rub it, don't make me hurt you."

This time I didn't argue, I just whacked him off as fast as I could.

For the second time that night, I made a horrible man come.

He gripped me even harder in the throes of orgasm, but as soon as he relaxed, I squirmed and broke free of his grasp. I took flight again, running out the first door I found, running through corridors and passing through more doors until I was outside, running on grass once more, running for my life again, just running, and running up the staircases until, at last, I burst into my room and jumped onto my bed as if it was a lifeboat.

This time, I didn't have to summon the tears. I sobbed. Men! What the fucking fuck!?

☙ Contaminated ☙

⌘

Islept all day Sunday, exhausted to death in my soul, but woke in time to eat some dinner and show up promptly for my shift that night. It was quiet at first, but Tommy soon drifted by. From the hangdog look on his face, I knew he'd already heard from Johnny.

"Are you okay?" he asked.

"No," I said. "Do you know what he did? Frank Sinatra? He fucking forced me to suck him off."

"Oh!" Tommy looked ashamed. "I'm so sorry, I had no idea...." He trailed off, not able to meet my gaze.

"He fucking raped me, Tommy."

"I'll talk to him," Tommy said. "You want me to talk to him? I will."

The way I felt right then, I might have responded more enthusiastically if he had volunteered to kill him for me. What would talking do with someone like Johnny?

"Yeah, sure," I shrugged. "Talk to him. It won't change anything."

"I'm really sorry," Tommy said. "I didn't know he'd be like that."

I wasn't so sure. He had to know that Johnny was psycho. If he didn't know, then he was psycho. Either way, all the trust was gone.

Our conversation was interrupted by the boss. Tommy quickly vanished and I got back to work. The boss often dropped by the switchboard to check on things. His manner was friendly and approving, but he barely said a word. He seemed like a lonely and haunted man, which touched my heart.

The last time he dropped by something peculiar happened. I had to pee while he was there, and excused myself to sidle past him into the tiny staff toilet in the hall behind the phone center. I hoped he'd stay in the outer office. The bathroom door was so warped, and the latch installation so gimcrack, the door gaped open when latched shut.

I was peeing away when I saw a shadow outside the door. The boss was standing right outside. Wait. Was he watching me? That was really creepy, and invasive, and mainly creepy but at the same time kind of exciting. Was he turned on by me peeing? I'd played some private masturbatory games involving pee. Did he have the pee fantasies too? How bizarrely interesting that would be.

I washed up loudly, and by the time I got out, the boss was back in the office, avoiding my gaze but with a tiny smile on his thin lips. Since then, he'd drifted by without stopping. Tonight he'd summoned the courage to walk into the phone center and form words.

"Would you come to my room after your shift and give me a massage?" he asked. This was the longest sentence he'd ever spoken to me.

"Well." This was completely unexpected yet not completely unwelcome. The timing sucked. But if I turned him down that could mean the end of it. He was homely, but it was the kind of homeliness that's sexy on a man. He had a huge jaw and sweeping forehead, he was enormously tall and bony, and though he looked like an antique to me, he was probably younger then than I am now. There was something indefinable about him that spoke to me.

Don't ask me what I was thinking, so soon after the traumas of the night before. In that moment, I felt like he needed me and god knows I needed someone right then, someone different from everyone else I'd met that summer. The boss certainly fit that bill. He was a big old softie, I could tell. It intrigued me that he'd spied on me peeing. I knew it was perverted on one level but on another level, which I didn't understand but could not deny, it really turned me on.

Maybe I was thinking: *I'll go anywhere right now with anyone who will take me as I am, broken and used and lost.*

More likely I was thinking this was life. Today's mission was to live life. Every day I woke up was another chance to get something right in my fucked up life.

Or maybe I wasn't thinking at all, and just following my lust.

I said yes.

Nothing happened or, in an alternate version of this reality, everything happened. You decide. I arrived to find he'd left the door unlocked. I rapped lightly and he told me to come in. He was already in bed and well-hidden by his blanket. Only his shoulders were exposed.

"Please massage me," he said.

I went to the bed and sat on him much as I'd sat on Leon during that teenage pot party, which now seemed like twelve centuries ago. I touched his broad naked shoulders. I'd never given a naked massage. His skin was surprisingly supple and soft. I rubbed him lightly. He moaned lightly. I rubbed deeper. He moaned deeper. He liked it.

I pulled the blanket down to the middle of his back, and kept rubbing and pummeling and working his shoulder muscles until he began writhing and groaning beneath me.

Oh! He was rubbing his cock against the bed. Oh!

I didn't mind one bit. It all felt too nice. He wasn't demanding. He was taking whatever I gave him. I pushed my fists into his muscles, enjoying his lurches as I straddled his back with my thighs. And then he groaned loud and his body stiffened in that familiar way, and I eased off him and sat beside him on the bed.

He didn't move. His face was still buried in the pillows.

"Thank you," he said.

"You're welcome," I said.

"Don't worry about locking the door," he said.

"Okay," I said. "Goodnight," I said. I let myself out.

That was it. An inexplicable sense of triumph flooded through me as I walked back. I liked riding his back while he came beneath me. I liked it that we didn't need words to communicate.

What I didn't like was that my legs were feeling wobbly and a wave of fatigue made the walk back seem longer than usual. I went to bed with a sick feeling in my stomach. The next day I woke up with a sore throat. I reported for work but couldn't make it through my shift. My back was killing me and the holes on the board looked fuzzy and surreal. The day after that I was too sick to go to work, and sent a message with my roommate to let management know. My roomie moved in with someone else, afraid of catching my germs.

It was getting really bad really fast but I didn't know what to do. There were no phones. No one came to check on me, no one brought me food, no one seemed to care. Time went by, days turned to nights and back again. I don't recall much else except that the entire time I sweated and shivered in bed, someone played the newly released album *Chicago* over and over and over again. I'd wake up from fitful sleeps wondering: *Is 250624 a date? A zip code?* And then incorporate the numbers into epic dreams that seemed more real than the reality I was living in my sickbed.

Around the third day, there was loud knocking. I thought it was another fever hallucination. Then the door creaked open. Lars peered anxiously at me. I was too sick to do more than pick my head up to look at him before dropping it back onto the pillow.

He was worried about me. When he saw I missed work for a few days, he asked around until someone told him I was sick in my room. It scared him when I didn't answer his knocks. He had keys to all the rooms, that's why he let himself in. Did I need anything?

I needed everything, I guess, because within a few minutes, he was helping me out of bed. I'd lost my voice so he stopped asking questions. Next thing I remember is sitting with him in a waiting room and then being examined by a gruff doctor who seemed angry at me. He told me I had a raging infection, I had to gargle with peroxide throughout the day and take a course of antibiotics. Recovery would take time. He thought I should leave the hotel and go home, where someone could take care of me. He was going to report my illness to the hotel.

I don't know how I got there – maybe my father fetched me, maybe someone at the hotel drove me back. One day I was in my bed in the Catskills, having fever delusions, and the next I was in my bed in Brooklyn, which in itself felt like a delusion but which, in a couple of days, turned out to be the grim reality.

I blamed Johnny. His sperm poisoned me. He had some horrible disease. He had contaminated me. That's why the doctor seemed so angry: he knew I had a sexually transmitted disease.

I'd disgusted him. I was just some hotel tramp who got what she deserved. The moment I was strong enough, I was getting on a bus and going back. All I had to do was go to the police and tell them I was 15 and Johnny would be cooked. Of course, if I told my real age, I'd lose my job, so I had to think about that more.

No matter. My real life was in the Catskills, where I was totally on my own, making all my own decisions. Whatever the ups and downs, it was MY life. I'd handle it. I was from Brooklyn. I'd seen a woman get killed and dragged down the street by a car outside my bedroom window when I was eight. I'd seen the neighbor's daughter get thrown out of a limo after being raped, dumped like trash in front of our building, when I was nine. I was tough. I needed to be on my own or life had no meaning.

When I got back upstate, I'd slow down my pace. I'd read more and flirt less. I wanted to get back to my fabulous switchboard. I loved that machine and the sense of power it gave me. I wanted to thank Lars. He was a true friend after all. I wanted to rub my sexy boss' muscled back again and ask him about that night he spied on me in the bathroom. I'd give Tommy what-for too, the bastard, setting me up like that.

I planned and schemed throughout recovery. Finally I was well enough to return. I called the hotel and spoke with the lady who'd hired me. They'd given my job to someone else, she said. I was a good worker, she said, but I was gone too long. They waited a week but then they had to hire someone else. It was the height of the season. She sounded genuinely sorry.

I couldn't believe it. I had to come back, I said. They still owed me money. She said it wasn't necessary. They'd mailed a check to me. I couldn't believe it. I was still in denial, planning what to pack to bring back with me, when a slim window-pane envelope arrived in the mail the next day, addressed to me. I didn't want to open it, but I did. It was my final paycheck. It was over.

I was grief stricken and panicky. I had a life to get back to. I had to get back. There were still a few weeks left to the summer. Anything was better than being at home. I felt exiled, condemned to life in my parents' home, the worst punishment imaginable.

My mother walked by and found me crying over the envelope.

"Don't be stupid," she said. "Your sixteenth birthday is coming soon. This is the happiest time of your life. You'll never be this happy again."

Getting fired twice in one summer. Getting assaulted twice in one night. If this was the happiest time of my life, I might as well kill myself now.

ೞ Maxed Out ೞ

⌘

As always, I recovered fast. Once the fever passed and I accepted that I was stuck in Brooklyn again, I became another version of myself.

I was harder and colder, and suspicious of men and their motivations. Being in situations I couldn't control made me paranoid. I knew I needed men for love, for sex, for stability but I could not imagine marrying one or promising to live with him forever. Men always wanted things from me that I didn't have to give. They had expectations of what women were and I was none of those things. Men needed to control women. They'd do anything to control them – bully them, whine at them, play them, and even kill them to get control over them. No one was ever going to control me, no one. No one would ever even know me, not fully. That box inside the box inside the box inside my brain would never get unlocked.

Little Miss "sure I'll give you a blowjob" was dead.

Within days of getting home, Max called. He didn't think I'd answer, he didn't know I was back, why hadn't I called him right away? He wanted to see me. He didn't understand it, but I had some kind of grip on him. He couldn't stop thinking about me. He needed to see me. How soon could I see him?

I wasn't sure, but his sexual hunger for me was sexy. He said all the right things, in his charming way. I decided to go. He felt familiar. I was bored. I wanted sex. He was safe and I felt so much older now. I had risen to his league, I thought. I wasn't his acolyte anymore.

He began thinking up little adventures for us, taking slightly larger risks. He took me on dates to quiet restaurants or into the city, where we could kiss and touch on the street, without fear of being seen by people we knew. At first, it felt like we were making progress towards a full relationship and we starting phoning each other every night.

One evening, he had me meet him at an unfamiliar building in my neighborhood, and took me up to an apartment furnished in old-people style, with stiff carpets and antique furniture. He insisted we have sex then and there, kissing me and pressing his stiff cock into my belly as he pulled me to the floor. It felt strange, kneeling on carved red carpeting, surrounded by furniture that grandmas sat on, and sucking him off while we said dirty words to each other. In his own bed, we loved smearing his cum around and drenching the sheets. Here he was fastidious about keeping his cum from getting on anything.

"You're tidy," I said.

"It's my parents' apartment," he said. "They're out of town. I wanted you to suck my cock on their living room floor." He guffawed, "Imagine if they knew!"

God, I wished he hadn't told me that. I'd had sex in my own parents' house, of course, but only by depressing necessity, not as a fuck you or, worse, an incestuous gesture towards my parents. He seemed to think he'd somehow sexually triumphed over his parents by perverting their rug. It put me on a tiny edge with Max that grew sharper with each passing day.

He didn't know that I wasn't the same girl he'd dated only a few months earlier. He didn't know I'd gone dark inside. We began having phone debates through the night, during which he'd tell me that men were more centered, more intellectual than women, and asked if I agreed that women needed men to define their identities. I couldn't tell if he was serious or only saying it to see if I went raving mad with indignation. Either way, I was supremely pissed.

Just before my 16th birthday, my mother began talking about throwing me a party. I was anything but "sweet 16" and didn't want one. Nonetheless, she called Robin and asked her to recruit attendees.

Robin quickly discovered I had a date with Max earlier that afternoon. This required her to spill the beans to me about my "surprise party" so I wouldn't miss it myself. I can't remember all the details, but through a baroque system of timed check-ins throughout the afternoon, relying on public telephones along Ocean Avenue, Robin managed to get me to the front door soon after everyone was assembled. I went from sucking Max's cock to eating birthday cake in under two hours. Robin and I were proud and smug about our secret achievement. No thanks to Max, though. For him, the idea that he could hold me back from others was a delicious little fillip to our encounter. He knew a party awaited, but kept delaying my departure with kisses and flattery, trying to pull me back into bed, as my irritation grew and I had to peel him off to get out the door.

Sometime in the late fall, Max suggested some novel fun – to invite Jerry Powers out with us to dinner. Mr. Powers was my homeroom teacher that semester. He was a shy, modest man, and reminded me of Droopy, with the same nasal voice and sad affect. It turned out he was a lonely bachelor who lived with his mother in Max's building and dined with her nightly. How awful for him, Max said. Wouldn't it be nice of us to invite him to join us some time? We'd go to a good Jewish deli, Max's treat. Jerry would enjoy the conversation and no one could turn down good deli, right? It would be fun, Max said.

I agreed whole-heartedly. Mr. Powers had always seemed intelligent and gentle, and someone I'd like to talk to. I couldn't wait. Up until now, Max had made a point of keeping me away from his friends because, as he once admitted, he was embarrassed to tell to them that he was sexually obsessed with a 15-year-old. They wouldn't understand, he said; they'd judge us. But I was now 16. Perhaps Max was finally going to let me into his life in bigger ways. I was going back and forth in my mind about him. He had a lot of great points but he just wasn't a nice person. He'd poisoned me against Feldman with sarcastic insights into Feldman's private relationship woes. He never seemed really interested in the things I wanted. If he was now finally taking me seriously, though, maybe things between us could change.

I looked forward enthusiastically to our dinner night. Going out with two educated older men who weren't related to me made me indescribably happy.

Max invited me over for pre-dinner sex, and then drove us to the deli. As we were parking the car, Max casually asked me to remove my bra. This was new. "Why?"

"I want to see the look on Jerry's face," Max snickered. "He probably hasn't touched a woman in years."

I was stunned. I didn't want to do it. I was supremely self-conscious about my breasts. In fact, I hated them. They were too big and bobbly. Max beseeched me. It was harmless.

"You've gone braless," he said, "it's no big deal."

Max knew the story of how I'd marched in the first big New York City Women's Lib rally the year before and decided to prove my commitment by going braless. In 1970, it was still a brave act, and though I was pathetically self-conscious about my boobs, as a purist, I vowed to overcome my inhibitions and walk the feminist walk. I still remember what I wore. I put on a pair of khaki chinos handed down to me by one of my amorous conquests, the baggiest shirt I had, a tan twill military shirt with big button-pockets in front and beaten-up army boots that I bought from the same funky military surplus store.

My mother screeched when she saw me. The idea that her progeny would leave the house without a brassiere incensed her. She flung her body across the front door, stretched her arms and legs into a human cross, and said I'd have to kill her in order to pass through without a bra. I explained my feminist philosophy. She was unmoved. Literally. She clung to the doorframe and screamed in that unsettling mélange of Polish and Yiddish curses. At that, I trudged resentfully back to my room, put on a bra, and finally escaped. As soon as I was out of sight of the house, I quickly pulled it off from under my shirt and stuffed it into my bag. I marched the way I wanted to march, the tits of my rebelliousness bobbling freely.

Max tried to play that angle.

"Think of it as a feminist statement," he said. "You're a free spirit."

I screwed up my face at him.

"Think of it as fun, it'll just be fun," he said. "It's just a tease."

I rolled my eyes.

"Oh, come on, what's the big deal? You've done it before."

He was right, it wasn't a big deal, I had done it before, but when I had, I'd done it because I wanted to. Not because some man pushed me to do it.

"Think of it," Max wheedled, "Jerry probably hasn't had sex in years. You'd be doing him a favor."

I stormed off. Did Max think I was that stupid? I went into the phone booth of a Chinese restaurant across the street, and dug for coins to call for a car service. Max followed me and squeezed into the booth with me.

"Oh come on." He hung the phone up.

He took me in his arms. He offered to take me home if I was really upset.

"Look, come on, please. Please don't go home. "

He kissed me in the phone booth, murmuring passionately. "I didn't want to hurt your feelings, you're beautiful," he said, "I just didn't realize you were a prude."

That pressed the magic button on my teenage ego. What?! Me, a prude?! Fuck that bullshit. I'll show him prude! I slipped off my bra and we returned to the deli.

Inside, Jerry was waiting for us and looked happy when we got there. He was as sweet as ever, and told me to call him by his first name. We had good conversations, too, but I felt like his Judas. I knew he was sneaking peeks at my boobs and that Max was eating it up every time he did.

I saw it all clearly. For Max, it was all about showing off my tits as his prize, dangling them before the horny sad-sack, and laughing on the inside. I felt so bad for Jerry, being treated as a fool and too naïve to know.

I couldn't stand it. I couldn't stand Max. I didn't want to be used. That wasn't what sex was about. Max wasn't liberated. He was corrupt. I was done. I went to the bathroom, put my bra back on and asked Max to take me home.

It was over with Max. It wasn't entirely Max's fault. He was an asshole, but he wasn't a dangerous asshole. I could have kept on having sex with him, and letting him introduce me to new restaurants and more in the city. I didn't have to be so serious about relationships, did I?

Well yes, yes I did. I had to be serious about the quality of the people I allowed close to me in order to survive. I had to run away when something didn't feel right. If I was wrong, so what – there would be someone else. But if I was right, then I'd just spared myself a lot of agony by departing when those red flags started to fly.

The truth was the truth and the facts were the facts, and peril to me if I ignored them. That was the lesson I learned from a summer that had started with a small lie.

❧ Old Glory on the Bay ☙

⌘

Ialways had places to go in my mind to protect me. As much as I enjoyed socializing with friends, I needed alone time too, time to live in my head without the distractions of conversation or the requirements of interaction, time to rebuild my sense of self and map out strategies for getting through life. This was as true when I was five as it is today. It was, I guess, my first coping mechanism for growing up with mentally ill people for parents and it's always served me well. I knew by the age of three that I was the only one who would ever take care of me. I couldn't quite believe my parents were really my parents. It was inconceivable that I was related to these supremely insecure, indecisive, crazy foreigners. It was more like I was forced by cruel circumstance to live with them, knowing my mother was capable of accidentally killing me at any time. I'll save the full family history for another book. Suffice to say, making my own decisions always felt like a matter of life and death.

By age 15, I was so adept at mentally escaping my environs that I could set the table, have dinner with my family, and get through a long evening of watching TV without being present on the inside. I had no choice about watching TV with them: my mom put the family TV in my room, reasoning that we didn't want to spoil the living room furniture by sitting on it. Thus the passage to sleep required a period of being held hostage in my own room by my mother's late night TV habits.

In my head I'd be continuing long conversations with more interesting people, or acting in a movie I just saw, or having an affair with a movie star who'd fly me all over the world and have sex with me in scenic places.

Every so often, my languid fantasy of an amorous encounter in Cannes would be interrupted by "Do you vant un epple? Here, khave un epple!" as my mother foisted a plate of fruit at me. I overcame such banal irritations to maintain the fantasy fugues for hours and even days at a time, while going through the motions of, and making the vocalizations of, someone who gave a shit.

If you asked me what I cared about then, I would have said things like world peace and civil rights. If you asked who I loved, I would have said my mother and father. I didn't know how to care about things yet nor did I love anything or anyone, least of all myself. I was the product of my home. I ran on duty and moral obligation. Those forces were deeply drilled into me. It was my job to be a good daughter. It was my job to give my parents the support they needed, not vice versa. It was also my duty to lie to them and to protect them from the truth about what I really thought of them. They had a "get out of personal responsibility card" called the Holocaust.

From the time I got my bike, my first summer in Sheepshead Bay, I lived on it as much as possible. I'd bike miles every day, stopping only if I found a place that felt "right." It could be a back alley, a garden, a place with a view, as long as it was far from the intrusions of maternal fruit plates. I rode all over the borough, looking for places I could be safe being me, without obligation or duty, without emotional engagement. I wanted to melt into crowds invisibly; I wanted to stand alone on a rooftop or a shore.

After the Catskills fiasco, there was nothing to do but get back on my bike once more. If I'd had a car, I would have never returned home. One day, I rode down to the docks of

Sheepshead Bay. I could never get enough of the Bay when I lived there – the glistening waters and old-fashioned fishing boats soothed me. I walked the bike to a dock's edge and sat down, feet hanging over the sparkling waters of the Bay. Seagulls were diving, the sun was on fire, and my daily life was a million miles away. If not for the homes lining the shore, it was like standing on the deck of a ship in the middle of a sea. It was a perfectly perfect moment of peace.

"Hi there!" A fisherman standing on board a boat tied to the dock called and waved.

"Hi," I waved back. My solitude broken, I got up to leave.

"What's your name?" he called.

"Glory," I said.

"No kidding!" He laughed and pointed at the name of his boat, which I hadn't noticed on entry. "Old Glory."

"OMIGOSH!" I giggled. "But I'm not old."

"How old are you?"

"Fifteen," I said, "16 in a couple of weeks."

"Awwwwww." He grinned. "Well, it was very nice to meet you, Young Glory."

He wasn't that old but he'd clearly spent his life on the sea, because his skin was like creased leather. From then on, until I started college, I'd roll onto the dock a couple of times a week to talk to him about nothing much and to stare blissfully at the water. He worked incredibly hard, which I admired. I'd sit there, smoking a menthol cigarette, while he swabbed guts off the deck and cleaned out smelly tanks. His life seemed simple and perfect. Every morning he took people out, and every afternoon he washed off the mess and prepared the boat for the next day. Sometimes he invited me on board and I'd explore the cabin and evade the gush of water from the high-power hose he used to wash off entrails. Once he let me handle the hose, laughing and instructing me as I struggled not to let it go. I knew I looked like a clown but it was too much fun to stop.

I'd never spent so much time with a person who wanted so little from me. See? There was good in the world. There were places I could just be, without it being complicated, with people who didn't have secret agendas. My girlfriends were all good people too. I'd lost my way in the Catskills, that was for sure. Now I wanted to be good too. I didn't want to be like my parents. I wanted to be able to be real all the time. There was only one small problem. No one would love me if they knew the real me.

One brutally hot morning, I thought I'd cool off by the ocean until the boats returned to harbor. I biked past the Bay to Manhattan Beach, and dropped my bike to run into the Atlantic in my clothes, planning to dry out on the sand. When I got back to my bike, a man was sitting next to it, wearing a tiny little bathing suit. I recognized him as someone I'd seen and briefly talked to before, though that last time he had more clothes on. He was sexy then. He was a lust machine now.

Paul was studying psychology at Brooklyn College. He was so brown from the sun he looked black or Cuban, but it turned out he was a Sephardic. He was several years older than me and from the moment we started talking, I knew he was extremely clever.

Not that his intelligence was really the focus of my attention on this day. He was nearly naked and my eyes were all over him. He was lean and slim-hipped like a boy, but buff like a man. His hair was as black and as sleek as an Asian girl's and his almond-shaped brown eyes burned with intelligence. He had a pointy face which, depending on the angle, either looked aristocratic or rat-like.

The more we talked, the more intense Paul became. Soon he was sprawled in my lap, while I sat there sort of awkward and stiff and yet amused and filled with lust for this naked stranger resting on my knees.

I pushed a strand of hair off his forehead. I stroked his long hair. I fondled his hard chest and abs. He was adorable.

"Do you want to be my girlfriend?" he asked suddenly.

"I can't," I said, turning away, embarrassed.

"Please be my girlfriend. You're so sexy and intelligent and nice. Be my girlfriend."

I was firmly resolved never to be anyone's girlfriend ever again. I didn't want to get too emotionally entangled with anyone. Sure, Paul looked great, but I didn't know what he was like inside. And he definitely didn't know anything about me that was real.

Paul kissed me. He kissed me so deeply, for so long, whispering sexy dirty things too. Everything I ever thought about boyfriends went away. Suddenly I wanted a boyfriend. I needed a boyfriend. Why? Because that kiss, right then, permanently erased the taste of Johnny and made me feel the way I wanted to feel when a man kissed me.

"OK," I said to him, "I'll be your girlfriend."

"You made me so happy," he whispered, fumbling in a hidden pocket of his bathing suit. "Quaalude? I've got enough for two."

‱ The End ⸂

⌘

To paraphrase Winston Churchill, "This is not the end. It is not even the beginning of the end." In my teens, every new adventure felt like the ultimate adventure until the next one began. And so the next volume of my memoirs will begin with the crazy adventure that Paul turned out to be, from his strangely sadomasochistic dramas in bed to the time he tried to set me up for sex with his gay brother, whether to cure him or simply appease him I'll never know. Meanwhile, my adult life with men had begun in earnest. Everything got even more complicated than I could imagine but, memory by memory, I will try to slice it, dice it and serve my sex history up to you.

By the time I am done with this literally voluminous memoir – bringing my sex history up to the gorgeous age when I had my first open and consensual experiences of BDSM –you may even understand the journey that led me there, and how truly un-predictable life can be when you are sexually free.

GLORIA G. BRAME, Ph.D., is a writer, blogger, board certified sexologist, and sex therapist. A widely-cited sex expert, Gloria is the author of several bestselling books about sex, including *Different Loving, Come Hither,* and *The Truth About Sex.* A professor at the Institute for Advanced Study of Human Sexuality she was named "Hero of the Sexual Revolution," by Exodus Trust. Gloria sits on the Board of Directors of the Woodhull Sexual Freedom Alliance, affirming sexual freedom as a fundamental human right.

CPSIA information can be obtained at www.ICGtesting.com
Printed in the USA
LVOW01s2229190215

427562LV00032B/866/P